Nashim Mesolelot

Lesbian Women and Halakha

A Teshuva with Responses

Rabbi Jeffrey Fox

with responses from
Rabbi Zev Farber, Rabbi David Fried,
Rachel Fried, Rabbi Aryeh Klapper,
Rabbi Ysoscher Katz, Rabbi Aviva Richman,
and Miryam Kabakov

I0211945

Ben Yehuda Press
Teaneck, New Jersey

Published by Ben Yehuda Press
122 Ayers Court #1B
Teaneck, NJ 07666
http://www.BenYehudaPress.com

To subscribe to our monthly book club and support independent Jewish publishing, visit https://www.patreon.com/BenYehudaPress

Ben Yehuda Press books may be purchased at a discount by synagogues, book clubs, and other institutions buying in bulk.
For information, please email markets@BenYehudaPress.com

ISBN13 978-1-953829-59-7

24 25 26 / 10 9 8 7 6 5 4 3 2 1 202400413

In memory of my father, Herb Fox, *z"l*

Contents

Introduction

April 3, 2023 | 12 Nissan 5783

כְּנֶגֶד אַרְבָּעָה בָנִים דִּבְּרָה תוֹרָה: אֶחָד חָכָם, וְאֶחָד רָשָׁע, וְאֶחָד תָּם,
וְאֶחָד שֶׁאֵינוֹ יוֹדֵעַ לִשְׁאוֹל.

*Concerning four children, the Torah speaks: The Wise one,
the Wicked one, the Simple one, and the One who does not
know how to ask.*

There are many interpretations for this section of the Haggadah, but what stands out to me this year is the defining label that characterizes each child. If they are defined as "wicked" or "wise," there is little room for multiple identities. The wise one is burdened by expectations of greatness. The wicked one can never be seen through a positive light.

In fact, a close reading of the question each child asks as recorded in the Torah reveals that the children are asking a variation on the same question. Perhaps then, there is really only one child with multi-faceted identities, revealing aspects of being wise, wicked, simple, and even unable to ask at different times. As Rabbi Yisrael Salanter (19th Century, Lithuania and Germany) explains: "Each of us contains all aspects of all four children." We do a disservice to our children when they are identified through a singular lens, when we cannot recognize their diversity of character. People become stuck when the fullness of their human potential cannot be recognized.

It is through this lens, where we all hold multiple identities, that Maharat proudly presents *Gay Women (Nashim Mesolelot): A Teshuva*, written by Maharat Rosh HaYeshiva, Rabbi Jeffrey Fox. The journey began years ago with a question that was posed: "Can a woman hold multiple identities? Can she be accepted into a traditional *halakhic* system that is core to her identity and proudly identify as gay? Can she be seen as a fully integrated member of the community?"

As a rabbinical school that values our *mesorah* and *halakha*, Rabbi Fox leads us through a deep exploration of Rabbinic and modern sources, compiling, interpreting, and framing the conversation of how our rabbinic sources understood gay women (נשים מסוללות) in our Tradition. The exploration began in 2019 with a convening in partnership with the Herbert D. Katz Center for Advanced Judaic Studies at the University of Pennsylvania, gathering together Maharat alumnae, academic scholars, rabbis, and women who were passionate about moving the needle on gay women's place in the Orthodox community. Rabbi Fox taught the texts, presented ideas, listened to feedback, honed his language, and over the next four years, wrote this response. The *teshuva* is meant to open a communal conversation, and it was important to us that we engage with and hear from respondents. We are grateful to Rabbi Zev Farber, Rabbi David Fried, Rachael Fried, Rabbi Ysoscher Katz, Rabbi Aryeh Klapper, and Rabbi Aviva Richman who have already participated in this conversation. In the coming months, we hope more will join.

Special thanks to Rabbi Dr. Erin Leib Smokler who shepherded us through the concluding stages of the volume with her brilliant editing and gathered the respondents. To Dr. Gillian Steinberg, who is a master of language. To Sari Steinberg for being an early reader. To the Maharat Board who has supported this project over these many years. To the students, alumnae, faculty, and supporters of Maharat who have been readers and real interlocutors.

And to Rabbi Fox, who wrote this *teshuva* because he could not operate in a world that ignores a large swath of our community; who intuitively understands that people seek to live an integrated life. Finally, to the women who inspired this project. Thank you for your guidance, patience, and leadership in bringing this article to fruition.

At the seder this year, may all questions, each child, and all people be welcomed around the communal table.

כָּל דִּכְפִין יֵיתֵי וְיֵיכֹל כָּל דִּצְרִיךְ יֵיתֵי וְיִפְסַח

All who are hungry, let them come and eat. All who are in need, let them come celebrate Passover with us.

Chag Kasher v'Sameach,
Rabba Sara Hurwitz
President and Co-founder

Nashim Mesolelot

A Teshuva

Rabbi Jeffrey Fox

Introduction: The process of answering any complex *halakhic* question unfolds in three stages: research, analysis, and decision-making. While all *poskim* engage in these three phases, they do not always present the stages as such in writing. This *teshuva* outlines the process so that the interested reader can gain from the research and analysis, separate and apart from the resulting decisions.

Research: In order to answer a question based on information, the *posek* must first gather data. This first step must be as objective as possible. Even the process of selecting sources and making decisions about which material is relevant has the potential to reflect individual bias. However, the honest *posek* can and must gather as much relevant material as possible, through careful research, to the best of his or her (hereafter: "their") ability.

Please note that the first section of this *teshuva* serves as an attempt to present the main texts from Chazal until the Shulchan Aruch within a very simple organizational framework. I begin with the three places in rabbinic literature that are directly relevant to the question of gay women and *halakha*, together with a few other texts from Chazal that are of import. Then I share most of the important material from the period of the Rishonim, focusing especially on the influential approach of Rambam. Finally, I outline the positions of the Tur and the Shulchan Aruch together with some of their key commentaries.

Analysis: Once the sources are organized, the *posek* must offer an analytical framework. This stage will reflect different modes of thinking. Some *poskim* seek to unpack material historically. Others are more interested in a set of conceptual questions. Some are driven by the desire to categorize based on authority. These different modes begin to bring individual bias into the discourse.

At this stage, material that may not directly refer to the topic at hand, but that provides different thought models, becomes part of the calculus. Different *poskim* approach complex questions using a range of methodologies. A simple and stark comparison is evident in the *teshuvot* of Rav Moshe Feinstein, *z"l,* and Rav Ovadia Yosef, *z"l.* Rav Moshe more heavily weighs Rishonim and very rarely quotes an Acharon. To be clear, Rav Moshe has done all of the requisite research, but his style of writing focuses the reader on the earlier material. Rav Ovadia gathers and presents in writing all the relevant sources — Rishonim and Acharonim — and only then shares his decision. The contemporary style of writing handbooks that summarize every position under the sun is yet another way to approach complex topics.

It is unfair to claim that Rav Moshe's style is better than Rav Ovadia's or that Rav Neuwirth's handbook approach is better than Rav Moshe's. They simply represent different reasonable analytic approaches to the world of *halakha.*

Decision-Making: The final stage, decision-making, is where the *posek* must be the most creative and where their own biases begin to show most clearly. For example, each *posek* would factor in the potential for extreme monetary loss differently. When does *kavod* or *oneg Shabbat* factor into a decision? What about a strongly held desire to take into account as many different approaches as possible? When is it the job of the *posek* to justify a *minhag* of the Jewish People, even when it appears to fly in the face of normative *halakha*? Can *kavod habriyot* be invoked in all cases?

This paper is organized around these three stages. My goal is to unpack the relevant material regarding women who engage in physical intimacy with other women in as objective a manner as I can. I then offer a few analytical frameworks for considering these sources. Finally, in the conclusion, I offer my own approach to this question as well.

II. Research

A. Rabbinics - Chazal

There are three main texts from the rabbinic period that serve as the basis for all future deliberations. One appears in the Sifra, and two come from the Talmud Bavli. There is also parallel material of import in the Yerushalmi, the Tosefta, and Vayikra Rabba. I present these texts as simply as possible, and with limited reference to Rishonim. At times, however, the commentary of Rashi serves as a starting point for ease of understanding. As a general rule, I try to read these texts with as limited a scope as possible, allowing others to make expansions.

1) The Sifra: מעשה ארץ מצרים — *Maaseh Eretz Mitzrayim* — The Ways of the Land of Egypt

Sifra, the *halakhic* Midrash (Tannaim) on Vayikra, plays a significant role in the subsequent unfolding of the question of queer women[1] in *halakha*. This Midrash does not appear in the Bavli or Yerushalmi but becomes important because of the Rambam's citation. The Midrash comments on the first three verses of chapter eighteen of Leviticus (an important chapter for this area of *halakha* in general). There we read:

ויקרא פרק יח, א-ג

(א) וַיְדַבֵּר יְקֹוָק אֶל מֹשֶׁה לֵּאמֹר: (ב) דַּבֵּר אֶל בְּנֵי יִשְׂרָאֵל וְאָמַרְתָּ אֲלֵהֶם אֲנִי יְקֹוָק אֱלֹהֵיכֶם: (ג) כְּמַעֲשֵׂה אֶרֶץ מִצְרַיִם אֲשֶׁר יְשַׁבְתֶּם בָּהּ לֹא תַעֲשׂוּ וּכְמַעֲשֵׂה אֶרֶץ כְּנַעַן אֲשֶׁר אֲנִי מֵבִיא אֶתְכֶם שָׁמָּה לֹא תַעֲשׂוּ וּבְחֻקֹּתֵיהֶם לֹא תֵלֵכוּ:

Leviticus 18:1-3
1) The Lord spoke to Moshe saying, 2) "Speak to the Children of Israel and say to them: I, the Lord, am your God. 3) You shall not copy the practices of the Land of Egypt where you dwelt, or of the Land of Canaan to which I am taking you; nor shall you follow their laws.

The Sifra begins its commentary on these three verses with the end of verse two: אֲנִי יְקֹוָק אֱלֹהֵיכֶם — *I, the Lord, am your God.* This is a somewhat awkward, seemingly tautological, formulation. The Midrash picks up on this phrase and reintroduces God to us:

ספרא אחרי מות פרשה ח סוף פרק יב

(א) וַיְדַבֵּר יְקֹוָק אֶל מֹשֶׁה לֵּאמֹר דַּבֵּר אֶל בְּנֵי יִשְׂרָאֵל וְאָמַרְתָּ אֲלֵהֶם אֲנִי יְקֹוָק אֱלֹהֵיכֶם - אני ה' שאמרתי והיה העולם. אני דיין. אני מלא רחמים. אני דיין להיפרע, ונאמן לשלם שכר: (ב) אני הוא שפרעתי מדור המבול ומאנשי סדום ומן המצריים, ועתיד ליפרע מכם אם תעשו כמעשיהם:

---

[1] While there was a time when the word "queer" was used as an epithet, it has been reclaimed by many LGBTQ+ people and has become a simpler way to refer to people whose gender and/or sexual identity does not align with heterosexual norms.

Sifra, Acharei Mot, *Parasha* **8 - End of Chapter 12**
The Lord spoke to Moshe saying, "Speak to the children of Israel and say to them: I, the Lord, am your God. I am the Lord who spoke and the world came into being. I am the judge. I am full of compassion. I am the judge who collects debts and I can be counted upon to give reward. I am the One who collected the debt from the generation of the Flood, from the people of Sodom, and from the Egyptians. I am also the One who will collect the debt from you in the future if you behave in their ways.

The Midrash presents us a God "full of compassion." That compassion is expressed in two ways. First, God is prepared to punish those who sin. Second, God can be counted upon to give reward. The linking of both reward and punishment to compassion is part of a rabbinic approach to the divine in our lives. Compassion does not mean simply forgiving everyone for their trespasses, but rather implies giving everyone what they deserve.

Just as God punished the generation of the flood, the people of the city of Sodom, and the Egyptians, God also will punish the Jewish People if we adopt their behaviors. It is not until the end of this section that we learn which behaviors are implied by this line.[2]

The next two *piskaot* of the Midrash describe just how awful the Egyptians and the Canaanites were. There is no single behavior paradigmatic of their evil ways, but both the Egyptians and the Canaanites are described as "abominable:"

מנין שלא היתה אומה באומות שהתעיבו מעשיהם יותר מן המצריים?
מנין שלא היתה אומה באומות שהתעיבו מעשיהם יותר מן הכנענים?

From where do we know that there never was a nation in the world whose behavior was as abominable as the Egyptians? From where do we know that there never was a nation in the world whose behavior was as abominable as the Canaanites?

---

[2] While there are some *Midrashim* that link Sodom to sexual licentiousness and promiscuity (see Tanchuma Vayera 12 and Tosefta Sanhedrin 13:8), their city's sin is more often described as injustice or inhospitality (see Ezekiel 16:49 and Bavli Sanhedrin 70a and 109a). Rabbi Steve Greenberg in *Wrestling with God and Men*, pages 64-69, clearly articulates this interpretation.

The phrase, "שהתעיבו מעשיהם - whose behavior was abominable" is particularly challenging, as it brings back that difficult word תועבה (*to'eva*) to describe their depraved nature. The section then concludes with the unpacking of the abominable ways of the Egyptians and the Canaanites:

(ח) כְּמַעֲשֵׂה אֶרֶץ מִצְרַיִם... וּכְמַעֲשֵׂה אֶרֶץ כְּנַעַן... לֹא תַעֲשׂוּ. יכול לא יבנו בניינות ולא יטעו נטיעות כמותם? תלמוד לומר וּבְחֻקֹּתֵיהֶם לֹא תֵלֵכוּ, לא אמרתי אלא בחוקים החקוקים להם ולאבותיהם ולאבות אבותיהם. ומה היו עושים? האיש נושא לאיש, והאשה לאשה, האיש נושא אשה ובתה, והאשה ניסת לשנים. לכך נאמר וּבְחֻקֹּתֵיהֶם לֹא תֵלֵכוּ:

The practices of the Land of Egypt... or of the Land of Canaan... you shall not copy. Could it mean that we may not build buildings or plant plantings like them? [No, because] the Torah says *nor shall you follow their laws.* I [God] did not mention [this prohibition] except regarding their laws (*chukim*) that have been established for them by their ancestors. And what would they do? A man would marry a man, and a woman would marry a woman, a man would marry a woman and her daughter, and a woman would be married to two [men]. For this reason the Torah says, *nor shall you follow their laws.*

We will return to the opening straw man argument that Midrash introduces,

יכול לא יבנו בניינות ולא יטעו נטיעות כמותם -

Could it mean that we may not build buildings or plant plants like them?"

in our concluding analysis. For now, let us make clear which behaviors are considered *maaseh Eretz Mitzrayim* (the ways of the Land of Egypt).[3] The Sifra lists four kinds of marriages:

---

[3] See the comments of the Korban Aharon of Rabbi Aharon Even Chaim (born in Morocco and died in Israel in 1632), אות ב and אות ג. He asserts that the Midrash is making a historical claim about the nature of Egypt. See also the fifth chapter of the Rambam's Shemoneh Perakim, which employs this concept as well.

1. A man to a man
2. A woman to a woman
3. A man to a woman and her daughter
4. A woman to two men.

The first (Leviticus 18:22, 20:13), third (Vayikra 18:17, 20:14), and fourth (Vayikra 18:20, Vayikra 20:10) marriages mentioned by the Midrash are explicitly noted as *arayot* in the Torah. What does it mean that the rabbis in this text linked the idea of a woman marrying a woman to three other relationships that the Torah forbids? Are we meant to understand that the author of this text believes that the level of prohibition associated with all of these marriages is equal? If that were the case, then it would be clear that the vast majority of the rabbinic tradition has fundamentally rejected the ideas behind this text, as will be explored shortly.

This Midrash sends a clear message regarding the Sifra's opinion of same-sex נשואין (*halakhic* marriage). In the rabbinic mind reflected in the Sifra, this type of relationship could only have been possible in the world of the Egyptians and Canaanites. To bring that kind of relationship into the rabbinic world is tantamount to assimilating non-Jewish behaviors.

2) Are Midrash Vayikra Rabba 23:9 & Bavli Chulin 92a/b Parallel?

A passage that appears in Vayikra Rabba must also be explored, as it appears, at first glance, to make a similar claim to the Sifra. In the classic printed editions (Warsaw), the Midrash reads as follows:

ויקרא רבה (וילנא) אחרי מות פרשה כג

ט תני רבי ישמעאל כְּמַעֲשֵׂה אֶרֶץ מִצְרַיִם... וּכְמַעֲשֵׂה אֶרֶץ כְּנַעַן... לֹא תַעֲשׂוּ וגו'. ואם לאו אֲנִי יְקֹוָק אֱלֹהֵיכֶם. תני רבי חייא למה אֲנִי יְקֹוָק כתיב שני פעמים? אני הוא שפרעתי מדור המבול ומסדום וממצרים. אני עתיד ליפרע ממי שהוא עושה כמעשיהם. דור המבול נמחו מן העולם ע"י שהיו שטופין בזנות. אמר רבי שמלאי כל מקום שאתה מוצא זנות אנדרלמוסיא באה לעולם והורגת טובים ורעים. רב הונא בשם רבי יוסי אמר דור המבול לא נמחו מן העולם אלא ע"י שכתבו גוּמָסִיוֹת לזכר ולנקבה...

Vayikra Rabba (Vilna) Acharei Mot, *Parasha* 23

Rebbi Yishmael taught, "*Like the ways of the Land of Egypt... like the ways of the Land of Canaan... you shall not do,* and if not, *I, the Lord, am your God.*" Rebbi Chiyya taught, "Why is *I, the Lord* written two times? I am the

One who collected the debt the generation of the Flood, from Sodom, and from Egypt. I [am also the One who] will punish those who will engage in their ways. The generation of the Flood was wiped out because they were drowning in *z'nut*." Rebbi Simlai said, "Any place where you find *z'nut*, destruction comes to the world and kills both good and evil." Rav Huna said in the name of Rebbi Yossi, "The generation of the flood was wiped out only because they wrote marriage documents for men and women."

This Aggadic (Amoraic) Midrash contains many of the same elements as the Sifra. It begins with a reintroduction of God as the One who punished the generation of the flood, the people of Sodom, and the Egyptians. We are then reminded that God will punish those people who behave like them. And then we are told that the major sin of the generation of the flood was זנות (*z'nut*), licentious sexual behavior.

It concludes with a statement by Rav Huna in the name of Rebbi Yossi that claims that the straw that broke the camel's back leading to the destruction of the generation of the flood was that they wrote גוּמְסִיוֹת לזכר ולנקבה. The term גוּמְסִיוֹת is a Greek loanword that refers to a marriage document.

The complete phrase, as it appears in the classic printed editions, seems strange. There is nothing problematic about writing a marriage document (*ketuba*) for a man and a woman. But some have understood this statement to refer to writing a *ketuba* for two men or two women.[4] If that is the correct understanding, then this phrasing would indeed serve as a parallel to the Sifra.

However, in his critical edition of Vayikra Rabba, Dr. Margulies notes that the correct text is, "they would write marriage documents for men and animals."[5] In addition, when this Midrash appears in parallel in Bereishit Rabba, the critical edition has the text of "men and animals."

בראשית רבה (תיאודור-אלבק)
פרשת בראשית פרשה כו
ר' הונא בשם ר' יוסף דור המבול לא נמחו מן העולם עד שכתבו גומ־
מסיות[6] לזכור ולבהמה.

---

[4] See the commentary of the Etz Yosef and Matnot Kehuna, in the classic Vilna Midrash Rabba, who understand that this refers to writing a *ketuba* for two men or two women. The Etz Yosef notes that the text of the Aruch is זכר ובהמה.

[5] See page תקלט, notes to line 4-5.

[6] See Theodor-Albeck edition vol. 1, page 248, note to line 6, where he also explains גומומסיות as marriage documents.

Bereishit Rabba (Theodor-Albeck), *Parasha* 26

Rav Huna said in the name of Rav Yosef, "The generation of the flood was wiped out only once they wrote marriage documents for men and animals."

This would explain why not only the people but also almost all animal life had to be wiped off the face of the earth at the time of the flood. Even the animals had been corrupted. It is also important to note that this trope appears in several other *Midrashim* as זכר ובהמה (male and animals).[7]

Another apparently analogous text appears in the Bavli Chulin 92a/b. There, we find a tradition that even though the *b'nei Noach* observed only three of the laws they accepted upon themselves, one of the three they maintained was not writing a *ketuba* for two men.

בבלי חולין דף צב עמוד א

וָאֹמַר אֲלֵיהֶם אִם טוֹב בְּעֵינֵיכֶם הָבוּ שְׂכָרִי וְאִם לֹא חֲדָלוּ וַיִּשְׁקְלוּ אֶת שְׂכָרִי שְׁלֹשִׁים כָּסֶף... (זכריה פרק יא פסוק יב). עולא אמר אלו שלשים מצות שקבלו עליהם בני נח, ואין מקיימין אלא שלשה: אחת (דף צב עמוד ב) שאין כותבין כתובה לזכרים, ואחת שאין שוקלין בשר המת במקולין, ואחת שמכבדין את התורה.

Bavli Chulin 92a/b

And I said to them: *If it is good in your eyes, give me my hire; and if not, refrain. And they weighed for my hire thirty pieces of silver...* (Zechariah 11:12). Ula said: These are the thirty mitzvot that the descendants of Noah initially accepted upon themselves, of which they fulfill only three: one (92b) is that they do not write a marriage contract for a wedding between two males, one is that they do not weigh the flesh of the dead in butcher shops and sell it publicly, and one is that they honor the Torah.

---

[7] See the Theodor-Albeck edition of Bereishit Rabba 26:5, Tanchuma (Buber) Bereishit 21 and 33.
בראשית רבה (וילנא) פרשת בראשית פרשה כו סימן ה] רבי הונא בשם רבי אמר דור המבול לא נימוחו מן העולם עד שכתבו גמומסיות לזכר ולבהמה. מדרש תנחומא (בובר) פרשת בראשית סימן כא] אמר ר' יהודה בר אידי לא נחתם גזר דינם של דור המבול, עד שכתבו גמיקיסוס לזכר ולבהמה. מדרש תנחומא (בובר) פרשת בראשית סימן לג] אמר ר' הונא בשם ר' אידי לא נתחתם גזר דינם של דור המבול עד שכתבו קמיסמסין (פי' כתובות) לזכר ולבהמה
Three of these four preserve Rav Huna as the Amora who transmits the tradition that writing a marriage document for men and animals was indeed the straw that broke the camel's back for the generation of the flood.

As Rashi[8] and Rabbeinu Gershom[9] explain there, even though the *b'nei Noach* were engaged in sex between men, they were not so brazen as to formalize such a relationship with a document. Though sometimes it is quoted in opposition to two women marrying, this text is irrelevant for our purposes, as it only deals with relationships between men where there is a potential Torah prohibition involved.

Neither the Midrash in Vayikra Rabba nor the Gemara in Chulin 92a/b reflects a Rabbinic approach to queer women. The Midrash is about bestiality, and the gemara is about men, not women. While these texts help us understand the Rabbinic approach to other types of human sexuality, they are not pertinent to the discussion of queer women in particular.

3) Talmud Bavli (Yevamot 76a and Shabbat 65a):
נשים מסוללות — *Nashim Mesolelot*

Two core texts present a rejected position of Rav Huna[10] regarding women who are *mesolelot*.[11] Rav Huna claims that women who engage in such behavior are forbidden from marrying a priest (or perhaps only from marrying the high priest). The Gemara never clarifies the exact nature of this behavior. However, it must refer to some kind of physical intimacy which could be understood as akin to sex between a man and woman in order for Rav Huna to claim that she may not marry a priest (or the high priest). I begin my presentation of the material with the passage in Yevamot 76a and then move to Shabbat 65a/b.

a) Yevamot 76a

בבלי יבמות דף עו עמוד א
אמר רבה בר רב הונא המטיל מים משתי מקומות פסול [משום פצוע
דכא]. האמר רבא לית הלכתא לא כברא [כבן של רב הונא] ולא כאבא
[רב הונא עצמו]. ברא, הא דאמרן.

---

[8] רש"י מסכת חולין דף צב עמוד ב שאין כותבין כתובה לזכרים] דאע"פ שחשודין למשכב זכור ומייחדין להם זכר לתשמישן, אין נוהגין קלות ראש במצוה זו כל כך שיכתבו להם כתובה.

[9] רבינו גרשום מסכת חולין דף צב עמוד ב שאין כותבין כתובה לזכרים] כלומר כשעושין משכב זכור אין כותבין להן כתובה.

[10] It is important to note here that Rav Huna was also the rabbi who taught us about the marriage documents being written between men and animals in the Midrash Rabba.

[11] I will generally try not to translate the word *mesolelot* because every translation that might be offered requires making a choice among the various *parshanim*. It is enough to note for now that this refers to sexual behavior between two women.

אבא, דא"ר הונא נשים המסוללות זו בזו פסולות לכהונה. ואפילו
לרבי אלעזר דאמר פנוי הבא על הפנויה שלא לשם אישות עשאה זונה,
ה"מ איש אבל אשה פריצותא בעלמא.

Bavli Yevamot 76a

Rabba bar Rav Huna said: One who urinates from two
places is unfit [as a man with crushed testicles]. Rava said:
the *halakha* is in accordance neither with the son [of Rav
Huna] nor with the father [Rav Huna himself]. The son
— that which we just stated.

The father—Rav Huna said: Women who are *mesolelot*
are unfit to marry into the priesthood. And even according
to R. Elazar, who said that an unmarried man who has
intercourse with an unmarried woman not for the sake
of marriage renders her a *zona*, this applies only to intercourse with a man, but lewd behavior with another woman
is mere licentiousness.

This piece comes in the middle of the Gemara's treatment of the man with
crushed testicles who may not marry into the Jewish People (פצוע דכא).[12]
Rabba, the son of Rav Huna, claims that a man who urinates out of two
holes is considered like a man with crushed testicles and may not marry
into the Jewish People. Rava rejects Rabba's analogy and also tells us that
Rav Huna, the father of Rabba, makes a separate claim that is rejected from
the *halakha* as well.

Rav Huna maintains that women who are *mesolelot* are not permitted to
marry priests. Rava says that this is not the accepted *halakha*. The Gemara
elaborates and says that even Rebbi Elazar, who holds that if a single woman
has vaginal intercourse with a single man for reasons other than matrimony
she is forbidden to marry a priest, argues that the prohibition only applies in
the case of heterosexual sex. However, if a woman were to engage in physical
intimacy with another woman (*mesolelot*), that is not even considered sex
but "mere licentiousness - פריצותא בעלמא."[13]

---

[12] See Devarim 23:2, Mishna Yevamot 8:2, Rambam Hil. Issurei Biah 16, Shulchan Aruch Even HaEzer 5.
[13] We will return to this phrase as part of a particular analytical frame. Suffice it to say for now that "mere
licentiousness" is not the same as "forbidden" and is also not necessarily the same as "permitted." In this
context, "mere licentiousness" is a way to say that this kind of behavior is not to be considered as though
it were *z'nut*, which has the power to forbid a woman from marrying a priest.

It is interesting to note two points regarding this text. First, Rav Huna is introduced to us as a rejected position. Before we even know his position, we learn that it is not the accepted law. Second, the Gemara raises the question of *nashim mesolelot* within the context of people who may not marry into the majority of the Jewish People. Rav Huna's stringency, which we reject, is about limiting the people whom this woman might marry.

For simplicity, I am going to offer Rashi's explanation of *mesolelot* as a placeholder until we can unpack what becomes a major debate. He says:

רש"י יבמות דף עו עמוד א, המסוללות
דרך תשמיש זכר ונקבה משפשפות נקבתן זו לזו.

Rashi, Yevamot 76a s.v. *Mesolelot*
In the way of intercourse between a male and a female, rubbing their femininity against one another.

For the sake of clarity, Rashi makes a specific claim about the behavior called *mesolelot*. He thinks that it is similar to intercourse between a man and woman because the two women rub their genitals against one another. We will address the detailed questions of what is included and excluded from *mesolelot* below.

b) Shabbat 65a

The Mishnah teaches us that young girls are permitted to go out on Shabbat (without an *eruv*) with strings pulled through their pierced ear holes and it is not considered carrying. The Gemara then introduces three stringencies of the father of the Amora Shmuel[14]. Shmuel was among the first generation of the Amoraim, which means that his father lived toward the tail end of the Tannaic period.

---

[14] The Gemara in Berachot 18b clarifies the names of Shmuel and his father. See Rashi on Chulin 111b s.v. *Aba bar Aba* where he refers to Shmuel's father as a *hasid*. This appellation is likely based on Shmuel's father going above and beyond the law (לפנים משורת הדין) regarding the maintaining of lost objects for more than a year (Bava Metzia 24b). The family were also priests. This biography does help to shed some light on the stringencies that Shmuel's father attempts.

ספר יוחסין מאמר שני סדר האמוראים אות האל"ף] אבא בר אבא הכהן אבוה דשמואל חבירו של רב, ובפרק אלו מציאות (ב"מ כד ב) שעשה לפנים משורת הדין שהיה חסיד גדול וכן בפרק כל הבשר (חולין קיא ב) אמר רב חס ליה לזרעיה דאבא בר אבא וכו' ופרש"י (שם ד"ה אבא בר אבא) דאבא בר אבא אבוה דשמואל חסיד גדול היה, וכן בפרק האיש מקדש (קידושין מד ב) חס ליה לזרעיה דאבא, אבוה דשמואל ולוי חברים (ברכות ל. ועוד הרבה) ולמה נקרא אבוה דשמואל שאמרו לו בלילה שנתעברה אמו של שמואל שיהיה לו בן חכם ובא לו על ידי קפיצת הדרך בלילה ההוא לאשתו ומיד חזר במקום שהיה שהוא רחוק משם והיו חושבין שלא היתה מעוברת ממנו ובא שהוא בנו כך שמעתי.

בבלי שבת דף ס"ה ע"א, "הבנות יוצאות בחוטין"

אבוה דשמואל - לא שביק [הניח] להו לבנתיה דנפקי [שיצאו] בחוטין,
ולא שביק [הניח] להו גניאן [לישון] גבי הדדי, ועביד להו מקואות
ביומי ניסן ומפצי [אריג של קנים] ביומי תשרי

Bavli Shabbat 65a

Shmuel's father did not allow his daughters to go out with
strings, and did not allow them to lie next to each other,
and he made ritual baths for them in the days of Nisan and
mats in the Euphrates River in the days of Tishrei.

The Gemara clarifies the first of Shmuel's father's stringencies:

לא שביק להו יוצאות בחוטין - והאנן תנן הבנות יוצאות בחוטין?
[החוטין של] בנתיה דאבוה דשמואל דצבעונין הוו.

He did not allow them to go out with strings. Didn't we
learn in the Mishnah that the girls may go out with strings?
The strings with which the daughters of Shmuel's father
went out were colorful ones, (and he was concerned that
because the strings were beautiful they would come to remove them to show them to others and carry them).

And now the *sugya* continues to elaborate on our core issue:

לא שביק להו גניאן גבי הדדי - לימא מסייע ליה לרב הונא? דאמר
רב הונא נשים המסוללות זו בזו (דף סה עמוד ב) פסולות לכהונה. לא,
סבר כי היכי דלא לילפן גופא נוכראה.

"He did not allow them to lie next to one another" — Let us
say that this supports Rav Huna, as Rav Huna said: Women
who are *mesolelot* are disqualified from marrying into the
priesthood? No, he [Shmuel] thought that they should not
learn [the pleasure] of another body..

The *sugya* is seeking an explanation for Shmuel's father's unusual stringency
of not allowing his daughters to share a bed. At first, the Gemara thought
that perhaps this was because Shmuel's father held like Rav Huna regarding
the damaged marital prospects of *nashim mesolelot*. The *sugya* rejects that

possibility and explains that the fear was that they would grow accustomed to sleeping with another body and build up a desire for physical intimacy with another. Rashi explains that the concern is that they will feel sexual desire for men.

For our purposes, this text does not add much more information regarding the exact nature of *nashim mesolelot* but simply reminds us that Rav Huna's position does not carry the weight of law. It is also interesting to note at this point that the Bavli does not cite the Sifra's concern of מעשה ארץ מצרים (the ways of the Land of Egypt). The significance of that fact will be explored below.

4) Tosefta (Lieberman) Sotah 5:7, Bavli Sanhedrin 69b, and Yerushalmi Gittin Chapter 8:3, page 48c

Before we move on to the Rishonim, the presentation of the rabbinic material would not be complete without reference to one other text that we find in reference to *mesolelet,* which may help shed light on its exact meaning. This *baraita* appears in three places, beginning with the Tosefta.

תוספתא סוטה (ליברמן) פרק ה הלכה ז
המסללת בבנה קטן והערה בה
בית שמאי פוסלין מן הכהונה
ובית הלל מכשירין

Tosefta (Lieberman) Sotah 5:7
A woman who is *mesalelet* with her minor son and he performed the initial stage of intercourse:
Beit Shammai say that she is unfit to marry a priest.
Beit Hillel say that she is kosher [to marry a priest].

This passage describes an incestuous encounter between a mother and her minor son. The Tosefta claims that if a woman is *mesolelet* with her minor son and he performed the initial stage of penetration, Beit Shammai and Beit Hillel debate whether this is considered sex such that she is prohibited from marrying a priest. According to Beit Shammai, such an incestuous act is considered sex even though the boy is a minor, and therefore the mother may not marry a priest. Beit Hillel claim that this act is not significant, and she is still considered fit to marry a priest.

Here we see that *mesolelet* is clearly sexual but does not include penetration. The formulation, "A woman who is *mesalelet* with her minor son and he performed the initial stage of intercourse - המסללת בבנה קטן והערה בה," assumes two separate acts: מסוללת (*mesolelet*) and then הערה (the initial stage of intercourse). If *mesolelet* were considered intercourse, there would be no need to stipulate that this incestuous encounter also included הערה.

This short section from the Tosefta appears in full in the Bavli in Sanhedrin:

בבלי סנהדרין דף סט עמוד ב
תנו רבנן המסוללת בבנה קטן והערה בה
בית שמאי אומרים פסלה מן הכהונה
ובית הלל מכשירין

Bavli Sanhedrin 69b

Our Rabbis have taught: A woman who is *mesolelet* with her minor son and he performed the initial stage of intercourse:
Beit Shammai say that she is unfit to marry a priest.
Beit Hillel say that she is kosher [to marry a priest].

However, when this appears in the Yerushalmi Gittin 8:3, page 48c, we find an additional clause of the debate between Beit Shammai and Beit Hillel:

תלמוד ירושלמי (ונציה) גיטין פרק ח דף מט טור ג /ה"ג
המסללדת בבנה:
בית שמאי פוסלין.
ובית הלל מכשירין.
שתי נשים שהיו מסללדות זו את זו:
בית שמאי פוסלין
ובית הלל מכשירין.

Yerushalmi Gittin 8:3, page 49c

A woman who is *mesaledet* with her [minor] son:
Beit Shammai say that she is unfit to marry a priest.
Beit Hillel say that she is kosher [to marry a priest].
Two women who are *mesaldot* with one another:
Beit Shammai say that they are unfit to marry a priest.
Beit Hillel say that they are kosher [to marry a priest].

It is first important to note that the Yerushalmi uses a slightly different word. Here they use מסלדות, replacing the second ל with a ד. This seems to be related to the word סולד or scald, perhaps through rubbing and creating friction.[15]

In addition to the question of incest with her minor son, the Yerushalmi adds the case of שתי נשים שהיו מסלדות זו את זו. We then find a parallel debate between Beit Shammai and Beit Hillel. Beit Shammai maintains that these two women are now considered unfit to marry priests while Beit Hillel holds that no such limitation is placed on these two women. This may explain why Rava was so confident that we reject Rav Huna's opinion in Yevamot 76a. It turns out that Rav Huna *paskened* like Beit Shammai, and Rava was simply codifying the law in accordance with Beit Hillel.

5) Yerushalmi Yevamot 8:6 (Vilna) page 9d (Venice)

There is one final text from the rabbinic period that has indirect relevance to our question. The Yerushalmi in Yevamot treats the *androginos*[16] question in a way that is different from the Bavli. We will return to the Bavli's treatment of this question at length below. I here present a short selection from the Yerushalmi, which again assumes the rejection of Rav Huna.

ירושלמי (ונציה) יבמות פרק ח:ו דף ט:ד

קידש אינן חוששין לקידושיו.

נתקדש חוששין לקידושיו.

נבעל נפסל מן התרומה בנשים וקשיא. רבי ניחא בר' סבא רבי יונה
בשם רב המנונה אפי' מין במינו כל שהוא וקשיא

נבעל נפסל מן התרומה בנשים וקשיא. רבי ניחא בר' סבא רבי יונה
בשם רב המנונה אפי' מין במינו כל שהוא וקשיא

אם זכר הוא אין זכר פוסל זכר. אם נקיבה היא אין נקיבה פוסלת נקיבה.
צד זכרותו של זה פוסלת צד נקיבתו של זה

Yerushalmi Yevamot 8:6, page 9d

If [an *androginos*] were betrothed [by a man], we are not afraid [that it is an actual] betrothal. If [an *androginos*] betrothed a woman we are concerned for the betrothal.

If [an *androginos*] is penetrated, they are considered unfit to eat *teruma*. And this is difficult. Rebbi Neicha the son

---

[15] See below in the Orchot Chaim under the definition of *mesolelot*.

[16] An *androginos* is a person with both visible male and female genitalia.

of R' Saba [and] Rebbi Yona in the name of Rav Hamnuna [said], "Even if an *androginos* has intercourse with another *androginos* in any way [they are unfit for *teruma*]." And this is difficult.

If an *androginos* is considered male - a male does not make a male unfit [by means of sex, to eat *teruma*]. And if an *androginos* is considered female - a female does not make a female unfit [by means of sex, to eat *teruma*].

The male side of this *androginos* can make unfit the female side of that *androginos*.

The Yerushalmi here assumes, without question, that if we were to consider an *androginos* to be female and two *androginoses* engaged in sexual behavior, they would not prohibit one another from eating *teruma*. The phrase: "אין נקיבה פוסלת נקיבה — a female can not make another female unfit" is a clear rejection of Rav Huna.[17]

It is difficult to make a global claim about *mesolelot* from this small *sugya*, but we can at least show that Rava and Beit Hillel, as cited above, are consistent with the position that *mesolelot* is not considered enough of a sexual act to prohibit a woman from marrying a priest or from having the right to eat *teruma*.

6) Summary of Chazal

What emerges so far from this earliest stage of our research are two distinct concepts: מעשה ארץ מצרים (*maaseh Eretz Mitzrayim*) and נשים מסוללות (*nashim mesolelot*). *Maaseh Eretz Mitzrayim* refers to a set of marriages, including that of two women, that the Sifra viewed as repugnant. *Nashim mesolelot* includes some sort of intimate sexual behavior between two women. We are also certain that when women are *mesolelot* with each other they do not, as a result of that behavior, become unfit to marry a priest. This is true according to Beit Hillel and Rava, despite the stringent positions of Beit Shammai and Rav Huna.

---

[17] This passage plays a significant role for the Rambam in Hil. Terumot 7:16. See the Ra'avad there as well as Mahari Korkis, Kesef Mishneh, and the Radbaz, who all struggle to make sense of the Rambam. There seems to be a fundamental debate about how to understand the word "צד — side." Does it refer to a particular physical organ or the different "sides" of one person who may have a doubtful status? Thank you, Rabbi Daniel Wolf, for bringing this Rambam to my attention. See also Tosefta Kifshuta Yevamot pages 94-96 and note 27 for Professor's Lieberman's comparison of the Bavli and Yerushalmi as well as the *girsa* question within the Yerushalmi.

It is significant to note that neither the Bavli nor the Yerushalmi refers to the concept of מעשה ארץ מצרים (the ways of the Land of Egypt), even though it would have been a useful answer to explain Shmuel's father's stringency of not allowing his daughters to sleep in the same bed. What we can say with confidence is that the rabbis thought that the marriage of two women was immoral and that physical intimacy between two women was not equivalent to sex between a man and a woman.

At no point do we find the word אסור, forbidden, in this context. This forbidding would not be a huge leap to make from the Sifra, but that language is not employed. Based on the flow of the *sugya* in the Bavli, we conclude that Rava believes that physical intimacy between two women is פריצותא בעלמא, mere licentiousness. This is certainly something to be avoided but does not imply a formal Torah, or even a rabbinic, prohibition.

B) Medieval Commentators - ראשונים

This material is much more diffuse and requires some organizing questions:
1) What is the definition of the word מסוללות (*mesolelot*)?
   a) Where does the word come from?
   b) What behavior does this phrase indicate?
2) How do we understand Rav Huna's rejected position?
3) What position does the Rambam hold, and how does he get there?

1) Mesolelot — מסוללות

a) What does this word mean?

Rashi, in commenting on the *sugya* in Sanhedrin, defines the word *mesolelot* in the following manner:

רש"י סנהדרין דף סט עמוד ב, המסוללת -
לשון פריצות.

Rashi, Sanhedrin 69b, s.v. *Hamesolelot*
In the sense of licentiousness (*pritzut*).

There is very little explanation here, but the implication is that the word refers to a kind of licentious approach to sexuality. פריצות (licentiousness) is the opposite of צניעות (modesty). This comment of Rashi is not meant to be a translation of the word but rather a description of a phenomenon. Rabbi Natan of Rome, in his 11th-century Talmudic dictionary Sefer ha-Aruch, defines the term סולל as "מַשְׂחֲקוֹת וּמִתְחַכֶּכֶת." The way that I understand these terms is "playing and rubbing," with a sexual connotation.

The Midrash Sechel Tov, written by Rabbi Menachem ben Shlomo around the middle of the 12th century, offers an interesting etymology of the word. He picks up on an unusual word that appears in the seventh chapter of Exodus in the context of the plague of hail. There, God tells Moshe to go to Pharaoh and give him the message of the coming plague. Within the message that Moshe is meant to relay to Pharaoh, he is supposed to say:

שמות פרק ט פסוק יז
עוֹדְךָ מִסְתּוֹלֵל בְּעַמִּי לְבִלְתִּי שַׁלְּחָם

Shmot, Chapter 9:17
You are still *mistolel* with my nation and do not send them free.

How exactly to understand the word *mistolel* is the subject of debate among many of the early Torah commentaries.[18] The Midrash picks up on this strange word and says:

שכל טוב (בובר) שמות פרק ט סימן יז
עודך מסתולל (שמות ט:יז). כלומר עודך מתחכך בעמי. ודומה לדבר בדברי רבותינו נשים המסתוללות זו בזו פסולין לכהונה. אשה המסוללת בבנה קטן, דהיינו המחככת בנה עליה, כלומר כזה המתחכך בכותל כי אתה מתחכך בעמי:

Midrash Sechel Tov (Buber) Exodus 9:17
You are still mistolel - that is to say that you are still rough with my nation. And it is similar to the words of our rabbis [who refer to] women who are *mistolelot* with one another they are considered unfit to marry a priest.[19] A woman who

---

[18] See Onkelos, who translates the word as כבישת which is quoted by Rashi. See also Rashbam, who thinks that the word comes from the root סולו, to build up, from Isaiah 62:10. The Ibn Ezra says, "כמו משתבח" from the root סלסלה based on Proverbs 4:8.

[19] See the commentary of Rav Yitzchak Arama, who refers to the same idea:
עקידת יצחק שמות שער לו (פרשת וארא-בא)[עוֹדְךָ מִסְתּוֹלֵל בְּעַמִּי. לדעתי הוא כאומרו עודך מתעולל לשון נשים מסוללות, מדברי חז"ל (שבת ס"ה א) אמר כל דבריך היו דברי צחוק והתול לבלתי שלח את העם אמנם על פי דבריך הנני ממטיר כעת מחר ברד כבד מאד לא היה כמוהו במצרים וגו'. כי זהו המופת החותך על היכולת המוחלט כמו שאמרנו:

is *mesolelet* with her minor son, which means that she is
rubbing her son on herself, which is like rubbing against
the wall[20] for you are roughing up my nation.

The Rambam, in his commentary on the Mishnah (Sanhedrin 4:7, which
we see at length below) asserts that the word *mesolelot* is related to the
word מסלול or path. The Orchot Chaim, which is analyzed in full below,
also offers a familiar etymology of the word *mesolelot* that appeared in the
Midrash Sechel Tov:

אורחות חיים הלכות ביאות אסורות פרק כז (בסוף)
... ולשון מסוללות מלשון מסתולל
פי' דורכות זו על זו.

Orchot Chaim, Biot Asurot 27 (end)
And the word *mesolelot* comes from the word *mistolel*,
meaning pressing one another.

The Meiri's approach focuses on the fact that there is no penetrative act as
part of this sexual encounter.

בית הבחירה למאירי יבמות דף עו עמוד א
ולשון מסוללות כאדם שדורך במסלה ואינו בוקע בעפרה כלום.

Beit HaBechira, Meiri, Yevamot 76a
And the language of *mesolelot* refers to a person who treads
on a path and does not penetrate into the dust.

He imagines a man walking along a path (מסלה), remaining on the surface
of the earth upon which he walks.

b) To what act does this word refer?

Any attempt to define the precise behavior begins with the comment of
Rashi quoted above:

---

[20] See Mishnah Bava Kama 4:6, which talks about an ox rubbing up against the wall and causing damage.

רש"י מסכת יבמות דף עו עמוד א
המסוללות דרך תשמיש זכר ונקבה משפשפות נקבתן זו לזו וכן המסו־
ללת בבנה קטן דסנהדרין.

Rashi Yevamot 76,a *s.v. Hamesolelot*
Like the way of intercourse between male and female, they
rub their femininity [genitals] against one another. Like
hamesolelet with her minor son (*Sanhedrin* 69b).

Rashi appears to limit the behavior to genital-on-genital stimulation in a
manner similar to sexual intercourse between men and women. He thinks
that the behavior of the two women is physically similar to the incestuous
encounter of mother and son as it appears in Bavli Sanhedrin 69b. This link
reflects, in part, that sex is defined in the world of *halakha* as the penetrative
act of a man's penis into a woman's vagina or anus. In order to make sense
of two women engaging in intimate behavior, Rashi imagines a heterosexual
encounter.[21] The Meiri echoes Rashi's language when he writes.

בית הבחירה למאירי יבמות דף עו עמוד א
נשים המסוללות זו בזו
ר"ל שבאות זו על זו אפילו פלטו זו בזו. אפילו היו חייבי כריתות זו
בזו אינן נעשות זונות בכך ליפסל לכהונה. שאין ענינם אלא פריצות
בעלמא. ולשון מסוללות כאדם שדורך במסלה ואינו בוקע בעפרה כלום.

Beit HaBechira LaMeiri, Yevamot 76a, s.v. Nashim hamesolelot zo bazo
Meaning to say that they come on top of one another and
even secrete into each other. Even if their relationship
would have [otherwise been forbidden with the] punishment of divine excision (*karet*) they are not, by this action,
made *zonot* [and therefore] unfit to marry a priest. For this
matter is just *pritzut b'alma* (mere licentiousness). And the
language of *mesolelot* is like a man who tramples on a path
(*mesila*) and does not break through the earth at all.

---

[21] See Rav Moshe Feinstein, in Volume Two of the Dibrot Moshe on Shabbat — סימן נג הערה לה — who
expresses this idea succinctly: "דלא שייך מציאות דתשמיש בלא איש" — the reality of sex does not exist without
a man."

Here the Meiri seems to be aware of the Rivan (below) and the Bavli and offers an interesting etymology of the word. In addition, none of these commentaries has made any reference to the concept of *maaseh Eretz Mitzrayim* according to the Sifra.

Rashi uses the phrase "דרך תשמיש — the way of intercourse" while the Meiri says, "שבאות זו על זו — they come on top of one another." In addition, the Nimukei Yosef, in his commentary on the Rif in Yevamot (Page 24b in the pagination of the Rif, s.v. *Hamesolelot*), quotes Rashi's language in full. The Ritva (Yevamot 76a, s.v. *Amar Rav Huna*) goes a step father and refers to the possible shearing of the hymen in order to help explain the position of Rav Huna.

The only other definition offered by a Rishon is that of one of Rashi's sons-in-law, the ריב"ן. Tosafot brings his interpretation:

תוספות יבמות דף עו עמוד א המסוללות

פירש ריב"ן מטילות שכבת זרע שקבלו מבעליהן.

Tosafot, Yevamot 76a s.v. *Hamesolelot*
Rivan explained — they place semen that they received from their husbands [into another woman].

The Rivan's idea is, on its face, surprising.[22] Why would he assume that there was male seed involved in the intimate sexual behavior of two women? I think this reflects the starting point that sex must include a part of the male body that is penetrating another body. In order to even entertain Rav Huna's assertion that these women are now unfit to marry a priest, it became necessary to add sperm into the equation.[23]

The next section in the printed Tosafot is a rejection of the Rivan:

ולא יתכן דבפ' במה אשה (שבת דף סה ושם) אמרי' שמואל לא שביק להו לבנתיה דגנין גבי הדדי משום דרב הונא דאמר נשים המסוללות כו'. ומשמע דלא היו נשואות, שהיו עדיין בבית שמואל.

---

[22] See the שיירי קרבן of Rabbi David Hirschel Frankel in his commentary on the Yerushalmi in Gittin 8:8 בבנה המסללדת ד"ה where he challenges the Rivan based on the Yerushalmi: If the child was only מערה there can be no semen involved. Rav Frankel was perhaps most famous for his (in)famous student Moses Mendelsohn. See the באר המלך of Rav Eldad Sabag on Rambam Hil. Issurei Biah 21:8, where he attempts to answer the challenge.

[23] The fact that we are talking about the priestly line makes the concern with the patrilineal line reasonable. According to the Rivan, we are clearly talking about a case of marital betrayal.

And this [the Rivan's explanation of *mesolelot*] cannot be right because in the chapter *Bameh Isha* (*Shabbat* 65a) we said that [the father of] Shmuel did not permit his daughters to sleep with one another, because of Rav Huna... And it appears from that section they were not yet married[24] because they were still living in the house of [the father of] Shmuel.

The Orchot Chaim,[25] at the very end of Hil. Biot Assurot, seems to refer to a kind of combination of Rashi's and his son-in-law's approaches with reference to the language of the Yerushalmi. He writes:

אורחות חיים הלכות ביאות אסורות פרק כז

פי' מסוללות: פרש"י מתחככות זו בזו מפני תאות תשמיש. ועולות זו
על זו ושופכת זרע להדדי. ולשון מסוללות מלשון מסתולל פי' דורכת
זו על זו.

Orchot Chaim, Hil. Biot Assurot, Chapter 27

The meaning of *mesolelot*: Rashi said, "rubbing against one another because of the desire for sex." And they come on top of one another and spill seed into one another. And the language of *mesolelot* comes from *mistolel*, meaning one presses the other.

The Orchot Chaim's description assumes genital-to-genital contact, as Rashi's does, and also presents seed as going from one woman to the other. However, unlike the Rivan, he does not refer to the husband's seed but rather to the "seed" of the women themselves.[26] He then refers to language as we

---

[24] The claim being made here that the daughters of Shmuel's father are not yet married is significant and the subject of a major debate, see below, page 39.

[25] This selection comes from the second section of the Orchot Chaim, which is generally paralleled by Yoreh Deah of the Tur. The Orchot Chaim of Rav Aharon HaKohen from Narbonne was published in the 1330s, just a few years before the Tur of Rabbeinu Yaakov ben Asher in the 1340s. Despite the Orchot Chaim's significance for understanding the *mesorah* of Provence, it was basically eclipsed by the popularity of the Tur.

[26] See the commentaries of Onkelos, Targum Yonatan, Rav Saadya, and the Rashbam on Vayikra 12:2 for the beginning of the treatment of the question of female "seed." Ramban and Rabbeinu Bechaye on the verse are also quite fascinating. In addition, Gemara Niddah: נדה דף לא עמוד א אמר רבי יצחק אמר רבי אמי together with the Rosh אשה מזרעת תחילה יולדת זכר, איש מזריע תחילה יולדת נקבה שנאמר אשה כי תזריע וילדה זכר there 2:2 (and the Ma'adanei Yom Tov). In the fourth volume of Asia תשמ"ג, Rav Avraham Steinberg has a pretty complete summary of the issue.

have it in the Yerushalmi. After we introduce the position of the Rambam below, we will come back to the approach of the Orchot Chaim.

Rashi uses the word "משפשפות" while the Orchot Chaim quotes him with the word "מתחככות." Both of these words imply one body rubbing up against another.[27] When the Tur offers a brief definition of this behavior, he writes:

טור אבן העזר הלכות אישות סימן כ
נשים המסוללות זו בזו פי' מתחברות זו בזו דרך תשמיש

Tur, Even HaEzer 20 (2)
Nashim hamesolelot with one another means that they connect with each other in the way of intercourse.

The idea that the two women are "מתחברות — connecting" to one another is new. The Tur appears to imagine that the sexual connection that is possible between a man and woman may also be a part of the sexual encounter between two women. By using the phrase "דרך תשמיש," he seems to follow in Rashi's direction that the act is particularly about genitalia.

The *mefaresh* on the page of the Shulchan Aruch in Even HaEzer 20:2 explains the behavior of *mesolelot* as "פי' המשחקות ומתחככות" (playing around and rubbing), without reference to any particular part of the body. The Levush offers a more complete description:

לבוש אבן העזר סימן כ סעיף ב
נשים המסוללות זו בזו, פירוש מתחברות זו בזו ומשפשפות נקבתן זו
בזו דרך תשמיש זכר ונקבה, אסור.

Levush, Even HaEzer, *Siman* 20:2
Women who are *mesolelot* with one another, meaning that
they connect to each other and rub their genitals one on
another in a way that is similar to male and female sex, is
forbidden.

Here we find the language of the Tur (מתחברות) that they are connecting to each other, as well as direct reference to Rashi's idea of rubbing their genitals

---

[27] The term tribadism refers to a particular kind of sexual encounter between two women in which the vulva is rubbed up against the body, typically the vulva, of the partner. Tribadism derives from the Greek word *tribas* (τριβάς) or *tribo,* meaning to rub.

together as though they are having intercourse like a man and a woman. As we have seen many times, the definition of their intimate behavior depends on its similarity to, or difference from, intercourse between a man and a woman.

There are two definitions of the physical act offered in the *Rishonim*. Almost everyone follows Rashi's lead and assumes that there is genital-on-genital contact in a way that is similar to intercourse between a man and a woman. The Rivan offers a creative read that assumes that there is male seed involved in the behavior. I am not aware of any literature in the Rishonim that addresses the question of ביאה דרך איברים or חיבוק ונישוק between two women.

2) How do we understand Rav Huna's rejected position?

Gaining insight into Rav Huna will help us to understand some of the broader questions at stake for the Bavli. The problem begins with an apparent contradiction within Rashi's commentary. When Rav Huna appears in Shabbat, Rashi claims that the two women who are now פסולות לכהן (unfit to marry any priest) are in fact פסולות לכהן גדול (unfit to marry the high priest) only.

רש"י שבת דף סה עמוד א
פסולות לכהונה - לכהן גדול, דלא הויא בתולה שלימה. דאף על גב דכהן גדול ביומיה לא הוה, הואיל ודרך זנות חשיב ליה, לאו אורח ארעא.

Rashi, Shabbat 65a, s.v. *p'sulot lakehuna* (unfit to marry a *kohen*) — To the high priest, for she is no longer considered a complete virgin. For even though there was no longer a high priest in the days of Rav Huna, since this is considered to be the way of *z'nut* (illicit sexual behavior), it would not be appropriate [it is not *derekh eretz* to marry the high priest].

However, when Rashi comments on Rav Huna's opinion as it appears in Yevamot, he writes:

פסולות לכהונה - משום זנות

p'sulot l'kehuna - because of *z'nut*

If they are indeed considered to be *zonot,* they are not only forbidden to the high priest but to all priests. The second half of the passage in Tosafot from Yevamot is responding to the contradiction. Tosafot writes:

תוספות יבמות דף עו עמוד א, המסוללות...
ולא יתכן נמי הא דפירש בקונטרס התם דפסולות לכהן גדול. דאע"ג
דכהן גדול לא הוה בימי שמואל מכל מקום מכוער הדבר כיון שנפסלות
בכך לכהן גדול. דהכא משמע דפסולות אף לכהן הדיוט משום זונה
מדקאמר אפילו לרבי אלעזר דאמר פנוי כו' מכלל דרב הונא משום
זונה פסיל להו.

Tosafot, Yevamot 76a, s.v. *Hamesolelot*

And also it cannot be what Rashi explained over there [Shabbat 65]) that they are unfit to marry the high priest. For even though there were no high priests in the time of Shmuel, nevertheless this matter is disgusting since they become unfit to marry the high priest. Because here it sounds like they are unfit even to marry a simple priest because of the status of *zona.* This appears to be the case from the fact that it [the Gemara] says, "Even according to Rebbi Elazar who prohibits a single [woman]..." we can infer that Rav Huna also claimed her unfit because of *zona* [status].

There are two important pieces to take from this short comment of Tosafot. First, Tosafot points out that referring to the stringent position of Rebbi Elazar, who claims that even a single woman who had sex with a single man without matrimonial intent is considered a *zona,* makes it clear that the question at hand is one of *z'nut.*[28] Given that we are talking about *z'nut,* the implication is that she is forbidden to all priests and not only the high priest.

In addition, there is a subtle shift of language in this passage in Tosafot that will be significant in future analysis. Rashi had described the behavior of *nashim mesolelot* as "לאו אורח ארעא - not the way of the world." When Tosafot is summarizing Rashi, he says that such actions are to be considered "מכוער - ugly."

---

[28] To understand the question of who is considered a *zona,* see Sifra, Emor 1:1 on verse 7, the *baraita* as quoted in Bavli Yevamot 61b, Mishnah Yevamot 6:5, together with Rashi on the Mishnah, Tosafot s.v. *shenivalah be'ilat z'nut* (Yevamot 61a), Rambam Hil. Issurei Biah 18:1-2 with Ra'avad and Magid Mishneh, Shulchan Aruch, Even HaEzer 6:8.

The fact that this behavior is "not the way of the world" or "ugly" leads Rashi to think that the women should be prohibited from the high priest alone. The implication of this statement is that, since she has not engaged in a forbidden sex act, she ought to remain permitted to simple priests. The act of *mesolelot* is not inherently forbidden but rather comes with a particular *halakhic* consequence due to considerations that do not apply to simple priests.

Tosafot in Shabbat refers to two possible readings offered by Rashi:

תוספות מסכת שבת דף סה עמוד ב, פסולות לכהונה

פי' לכהונה גדולה דלאו בתולה שלימה היא ואף על גב דכהן גדול
בימי שמואל לא הוה היה מחמיר וי"מ משום זונה ופסולות אף לכהן
הדיוט. וכן משמע בפ' הערל (יבמות עו.) דקאמר התם "לית הלכתא
[לא כברא ולא] כאבא (עד דקאמר) [וקאמר] ואפילו לרבי אלעזר
דאמר פנוי הבא על הפנויה שלא לשם אישות עשאה זונה" כו' משמע
דטעמא משום זונה.

Tosafot, Shabbat 65a s.v. *p'sulot lakehuna*

Meaning that she is prohibited from marrying the high priest because she is no longer considered a full virgin. And even though there was no high priest in the days of Shmuel, he was stringent. And some people explain that she is unfit as a *zona* and therefore also prohibited even from marrying a simple priest. And so it appears from the *Yevamot* 76a for it says, "The laws does not accord with the father or the son... and even according to Rebbi Elazar who said that if a single man and single woman have intercourse not for the sake of marriage she is considered a *zona*" it sounds that the reason is because she is considered a *zona*.

Here, Tosafot refers to the position of Rashi without attribution and simply says that, even though there were no high priests around in those days, Shmuel's father chose to be stringent. Then Tosafot refers to the more commonly held position that, according to Rav Huna, she would be prohibited from marrying any priest.

It is interesting to note that when the Tosafot HaRosh in Shabbat quotes this same debate, he names Rashi and gives him a particular interlocutor:

תוספות הרא"ש שבת דף סה עמוד ב
נשים המסוללות זו בזו פסולות לכהונה, פרש"י לכהן גדול דלא הויא
בתולה שלימה. וריב"א פי' אפי' לכהן הדיוט פסולה משום זונה.

Tosafot HaRosh, Shabbat 65b, s.v. *Nashim hamesolelot zo bazo*

Rashi explained that she is forbidden [only] to the high priest for she is [no longer considered] a complete virgin. And the Riva explained that [she is unfit from marrying] even a simple priest because she is considered a *zona*.

Here Rashi is presented as debating with one of the earliest named *Ba'alei HaTosafot*, Rabbi Yitzchak ben Asher HaLevi, who lived in the 11th century in Speyer.[29] The Riva, like the majority of those who came after him, held that, according to Rav Huna, *nashim mesolelot* are meant to be unfit to all priests and not just the high priest.

The Ramban,[30] Rashba, Ran, and Ritva[31] (Shabbat 65a s.v. *Nashim hamesolelot*) are all puzzled by Rashi's limitation of the פסול only to the high priest. All four are bothered first by the language of the *sugya* here in Shabbat. If Rav Huna meant that these women would be unfit only for the high priest, he should have said so. Simply saying "פסולות לכהונה" implies forbiddenness to all priests. In addition, like Tosafot, they point out that the *sugya* in Yevamot refers to Rebbi Elazar, implying that the status in conversation is one of *zona* and not *be'ula*.

---

[29] He was the son-in-law of R. Elyakim ben Meshulum, who was Rashi's fellow student at the Yeshivot of Worms and Mainz. The Riva and the Rivan, who both figure in this debate, likely knew one another and lived at the same time.

[30] Ramban, Rashba, and Ritva are also bothered by an implicit contradiction between the *mesolelot* sugya in Yevamot (76a) and another passage in Yevamot (59b, 60a) regarding the prohibition of a priest to marry a woman who had been seduced or, God forbid, raped. On 76a, the Gemara aligns the position of Rav Huna on *mesolelot* with the stringency of Rebbi Elazar regarding the prohibition of a single woman who engaged in non-marital intercourse to marry a priest because she is considered a *zona*. Here the Gemara seems to take for granted that Rav Huna agrees with Rebbi Elazar and goes one step further. However, the Gemara on 60a appears to think that Rav Huna cannot agree with Rebbi Elazar. This question will ultimately animate the Aruch LaNer cited below.

[31] See also the comment of Rabbi Yehuda Yerucham Fischel Perelow (d. Jerusalem, 1937) in his exhaustive commentary on the Sefer HaMitzvot of Rav Saadia Gaon לאוין ל"ת רסד רסה in the paragraph beginning, "וכן נראה ראיה מדאמרינן בפרק הערל" where he unpacks the Ramban and Ritva.

The Ritva and Ramban[32] both conclude that Rav Huna does not limit his *chumra* of *nashim mesolelot* only to the parameters of Rebbi Elazar, who maintains that a single woman who has sex with a single man is prohibited from marrying a priest. Rather, even according to the Chakhamim, who reject Rebbi Elazar's stringency, Rav Huna would still maintain that *nashim mesolelot* are prohibited from marrying any priest. Rav Huna, therefore, must consider the behavior of *mesolelot* as close enough to *halakhic* sex that those who engage in it are considered *zonot*.

They go on to clarify that Rava, who rejects Rav Huna, holds that even according to Rebbi Elazar, *nashim mesolelot* are not prohibited from marrying any priest because we cannot claim that *halakhic* sex took place between two women. For Rava, who represents the Gemara's conclusion, the act of *mesolelot* is not itself inherently prohibited.

3) What did the Rambam decide, and how did he get there?

In a lengthy comment on the Mishnah in Sanhedrin 7:4, Rambam offers the following introduction:

פירוש המשנה לרמב"ם מסכת סנהדרין פרק ז משנה ד
והנה מקום אתי להזכיר בו כללים רבים מאד מעניני העריות ואף על
פי שהם מפוזרים בכמה מקומות במשנה וכבר ביארנו כל כלל מהם
במקומו, אלא שאני מקבצם כאן כדי שיהו כולם במקום אחד למי
שירצה לעיין בהם, ואזכיר גם ענינים שלא נתבארו במשנה כדי שיהא
הענין שלם כולו...

Rambam, Commentary on the Mishnah, Sanhedrin 7:4
And behold this is a place for me to mention many general rules regarding the topic of *arayot* (forbidden sexual relationships). And even though they are spread in many places around the Mishnah and we have already explained each rule in its place, nonetheless I have gathered them all together here in order that they can all be in one place for someone who wants to look into them. And I will also men-

---

[32] See the Gilyonei HaShas of Rav Yosef Engle on Yevamot 76a, where he pushes the Ramban's read of Rav Huna. If indeed a women who is *mesolelet* is considered a *zona*, Rav Engle asks about the following case: אשה כהנת המסללת בנסללת (the daughter of a priest who is *mesolelet* with a woman who has already been *mesalelet* before) — has she violated two potential prohibitions: 1) *mesolelet* and, 2) sex with a *zona*?

tion matters that have not been clarified in the Mishnah so that the topic can be complete...

After working through the basic Torah categories of forbidden sexual behavior, he says:

...וכן אותו המעשה המגונה הקורה בין הנשים ששוכבות זו את זו, הוא מעשה מתועב, אבל אין בו עונש לא מן התורה ולא מדרבנן. ואין שום אחת מהן נקראת זונה. ואינה נאסרת על בעלה. ואינה נאסרת לכהן. וזה הוא שקוראים אותו חכמים נשים המסוללות זו בזו. והוא נגזר מן מסלול שהוא הדרך. ואף על פי שאין בזה עונש כבר מנו מעשה זה מכלל תועבות המצריים ואמרו בפירוש מעשה ארץ מצרים. מה היו עושין? איש נושא איש, ואשה נושאה אשה, ואשה נשאת לשני אנשים.

And also that offensive act that happens between women who lie one with the other - and it is an abominable act - but it has no punishment from the Torah or from the Rabbis. And neither of them is called a *zona*. And she is not forbidden on her husband. And she is not forbidden from marrying a priest. And this is what the Sages call *nashim mesolelot*. And it is from the root *maslool*, which means *path*. And even though this has no punishment, the rabbis have already counted this among the abominable ways of the Egyptians. And they have clearly called this *maaseh Eretz Mitzrayim*. And what would they do? A man would marry a man, a woman would marry a woman, and a woman would be married to two men.

Here Rambam refers to sexual behavior between two women as "מגונה - offensive" and "מתועב — abominable" and makes a direct link between the Bavli's language of נשים מסוללות (*nashim mesolelot*) and מעשה ארץ מצרים (*maaseh Eretz Mitzrayim*). He also makes clear that this kind of sexual intimacy does not carry with it a punishment — either from the Torah or from the rabbis — and that neither woman is considered a *zona*, nor is either prohibited from being with her husband or from marrying a priest. It is important to note that the word אסור (forbidden) is absent from this paragraph.

In his ordering and counting of the mitzvot, Rambam also refers to this same kind of behavior. In negative mitzvah number 353, he begins:

ספר המצוות לרמב״ם מצות לא תעשה שנג
והמצוה השנ״ג היא שהזהירנו מקרוב לאחת מכל אלו העריות ואפילו
בלא ביאה. כגון חבוק ונשיקה והדומה להם מפעולות הזנות...

Sefer HaMitzvot, Negative Commandment Number 353
And the 353rd *mitzvah* is that we have been warned to not
[even] come close to any one of the *arayot*, even without
intercourse. [This would include things] like hugging and
kissing and things that are similar to that...

He then goes on to quote the Midrash from the Sifra:

ולשון ספרא יכול לא יבנו בתים ולא יטעו כרמים כמותם? תלמוד
לומר ובחוקותיהם לא תלכו. לא אמרתי אלא בחוקים החקוקים להם
ולאבותיהם. ושם אמרו מה היו עושים האיש נושא איש ואשה נושאה
אשה ואשה נשאת לשני אנשים. הנה כבר התבאר כי אלו הלאוין שהם
כמעשה ארץ מצרים וכמעשה ארץ כנען לא תעשו הם אזהרה מבעילת
כל העריות על הכלל.

And the language of the Sifra: "Could it mean that we
may not build buildings or plant plantings like them?
[No, because] the Torah says *nor shall you follow their
laws.* I [God] did not mention [this prohibition] except
regarding their laws (*chukim*) that have been established
for them by their ancestors." And they continued there
and said, "And what would they do? A man would marry
a man, and a woman would marry a woman, and a woman
would be married to two [men]." And behold it has already
been explained that these negative prohibitions — which
are *k'maaseh Eretz Mitzrayim u'k'maaseh Eretz Canaan
lo taasu* — they are a warning against intercourse with all
arayot in general.

Here the prohibition of כמעשה ארץ מצרים וכמעשה ארץ כנען (*maaseh Eretz Mitzrayim*) takes on additional significance. This concept is no longer limited
to four particular marriages but comes to include a general prohibition of
all activities that have any trace of *arayot*. While Rambam raises the Sifra's
prohibition for a woman to marry another woman, here *nashim mesolelot*
is not mentioned at all.

The Rambam clarifies the full combination and explicit prohibition only in the Mishneh Torah:

רמב"ם הלכות איסורי ביאה פרק כא הלכה ח
נשים המסוללות זו בזו אסור וממעשה מצרים הוא שהוזהרנו עליו
שנאמר כמעשה ארץ מצרים לא תעשו. אמרו חכמים מה היו עושים?
איש נושא איש ואשה נושא אשה, ואשה נשאת לשני אנשים. אף על
פי שמעשה זה אסור אין מלקין עליו. שאין לו לאו מיוחד והרי אין שם
ביאה כלל. לפיכך אין נאסרות לכהונה משום זנות. ולא תיאסר אשה
על בעלה בזה שאין כאן זנות. וראוי להכותן מכת מרדות הואיל ועשו
איסור. ויש לאיש להקפיד על אשתו מדבר זה ומונע הנשים הידועות
בכך מלהכנס לה ומלצאת היא אליהן.

Rambam, Mishneh Torah, The Laws of Forbidden Sexual Relations, Chapter 28 *Halakha* 8

Women who are *mesolelot* one with another — This is for-bidden from *maaseh Eretz Mitzrayim* that we have been warned about, as it is written, "Do not copy the practices of the Land of Egypt. The *Chakhamim* asked, "What would they do? A man would marry a man, and a woman would marry a woman, and a woman would be married to two [men]." And even though it is forbidden, the court does not give lashes for it, because there is no specific prohibi-tion and there is no actual intercourse. Therefore she is not prohibited from marrying a priest due to *z'nut* and she is not prohibited from [being with] her husband [because] of this, because there is no [issue of] *z'nut* here. And it is appropriate to hit them with blows of rebellion, since they have committed a violation. And a man should be careful to keep his wife away from this matter. And he should stop women who are known to engage in this behavior from coming into his home and keep his wife away from going out to them.

In the Mishneh Torah, Rambam works with the combination of נשים מסוללות and מעשה ארץ מצרים that he originated in his commentary on the Mishnah in Sanhedrin, and he adds the missing language of אסור (forbidden) from his own מנין המצוות (counting of the commandments). This formulation sets the stage for nearly every subsequent code of Jewish law.

Nashim Mesolelot

There is an interesting progression in the Rambam's works from his commentary on the Mishnah to his Mishneh Torah. In his comment on Sanhedrin 7:4, he describes the physical act of *mesolelot* as "את זו שוכבות זו — lying one with another." He makes clear about this kind of behavior that there is no prohibition, punishment or consequence. He concludes the paragraph with a reference to the Sifra and *maaseh Eretz Mitzrayim* as types of relationships that the rabbis despised.

In his Sefer HaMitzvot, he refers to the idea of *maaseh Eretz Mitzrayim* but does not mention the concept of *mesolelot* even once. In the Mishneh Torah, he goes one step further and defines *nashim mesolelot* as derivative of *maaseh Eretz Mitzrayim*:

נשים המסוללות זו בזו אסור וממעשה מצרים הוא שהוזהרנו עליו

Nashim hamesolelot are forbidden, and it is from *maaseh Eretz Mitzrayim*, which we have been forewarned about.

The Rambam does something quite radical. He takes a concept from the Bavli (*nashim mesolelot*) and subsumes it under a concept from the Sifra (*maaseh Eretz Mitzrayim*). This is an unusual way to read the corpus of rabbinic literature. He is the first — and almost the only — Rishon to make such a claim. While one must always contend with the Rambam because of his stature, it is important to appreciate the ways in which this is a departure from the Bavli as the authoritative text of *halakha*.

The Magid Mishneh, in explaining Rambam, points out that he combines the Bavli and the Sifra. While the Midrash referred to four marriage relationships as *maaseh Eretz Mitzrayim*, Rambam quotes this Midrash here only regarding two women. He does not mention this idea of the Sifra in any other context.[33]

The Magid Mishneh concludes by quoting Rashi and Rivan:

---

[33] See Yerushalmi, Sukkah 5:1 (in the name of רשב"י) and Mechilta d'Rebbi Yishmael, Beshalach, Masechta d'Vayehi, *Parasha* 2 (toward the end, with no attribution). See Rambam Hil. Melachim 5:8, where he uses the phrase *maaseh Eretz Mitzrayim* within his discussion regarding the prohibition of living in Egypt. In addition, see Sefer HaMitzvot negative commandment 46. The Radvaz on Hil. Melachim 5:8 is important, as he also lived in Egypt. The Kaftor VaFerach, Chapter 5, refers to a tradition that Rambam signed his letters, "I, Moshe, who violates three prohibitions every day," one of which was living in Egypt. However, Rav Ovadia in Yechave Daat 3:81 disputes this notion. It is interesting that the narrative conclusion of the Nevi'im describes the assassination of Gedalia and the return of the Jewish People to Egypt, a complete reversal of the book of Exodus (See II Kings 25:25-26).

מגיד משנה הלכות איסורי ביאה פרק כא הלכה ח
ופי' ריב"ן ורש"י ז"ל מסוללות שדיין שכבת זרע להדדי.
ודין המכת מרדות שכתב רבינו פשוט הוא.

Magid Mishneh Rambam, Commentary on the Mishnah, Sanhedrin 7:4

And the Rivan and Rashi, of blessed memory, explained *mesolelot* as one [placing] semen in the other. And the judgment of Rabbinic lashes that Rambam wrote is clear.

It is strange that he quotes Rashi and Rivan together, as though Rashi agrees with Rivan's approach.[34] One can not overstate the influence of the Rambam in this area of *halakha* in particular as well as in the general flow of the history of *halakha*. His creative reading of the Bavli in the light of the Sifra sets the tone for many subsequent *poskim*. However, his was a minority position in the Rishonim and is simply not the only — or frankly, the best — way to read the Bavli.

C) Tur / Shulchan Aruch — טור ושו"ע

Rabbeinu Yaakov ben Asher (d. 1343) in his Tur, Even HaEzer, Hil. Ishut Number 20[35], quotes the Rambam almost in full. The only substantive addition that he makes is his attempt to define the particular act of *mesolelot*. He writes:

טור אבן העזר הלכות אישות סימן כ
נשים המסוללות זו בזו פי' מתחברות זו בזו דרך תשמיש אסור וזה
מעשה ארץ מצרים שהוזהרנו עליו שנאמר כמעשה ארץ מצרים אשר
ישבתם בה לא תעשו ואמרו חכמים ז"ל מה היו עושים? איש נושא

---

[34] See the חדות יעקב חלק אב"ע סימן מג of Rabbi Yaakov Hadas, who served as a rebbe and rosh yeshiva at Porat Yosef in Jerusalem and was the teacher of Rabbi Ovadia Yosef and Ben Zion Abba Shaul. In the midst of a lengthy *teshuva* in opposition to artificial insemination, he refers to this passage in the Magid Mishneh and wonders if perhaps there was a different text of Rashi that the Magid Mishneh had. Part of the conclusion of his *teshuva* reads as follows: דדוקא במטילות ש"ז שקבלו מבעליהן הוא דאמר ר"ה דפסולות לכהונה הא אם לא היו נשואות אינן נפסלות וכן לענין מסקנא דלא נפסלות אלא דהוי פריצותא לפי פי' ריב"ן הוא דוקא בנשואות אבל בפנויות אין אפילו פריצותא. He notes here that, according to the Rivan, if the two women are single, *nashim mesolelot* is not even considered *pritzut*.

[35] The Rif, Yevamot 24b (of the Rif's pagination), simply quotes the Gemara in full. The Nimukei Yosef there refers to Rashi's understanding of the physical behavior as rubbing genitals. The Rosh in Yevamot 8:2 quotes the Gemara as well. Rabbeinu Yeruchum in Toldot Adam V'Chava Netiv 23 *Chelek* 4 (page 199c) simply refers to *nashim mesolelot* as *pritzut* and notes that they are permitted to priests. In addition, the Semag, negative commandment 126, quotes the Rambam in full.

33

איש ואשה נושאת אשה ואשה נשאת לשני אנשים. ואף על פי שהוא
אסור אין לוקין עליו ואין האשה נאסרת על בעלה בכך אבל ראוי
לנדותה ולהכותה מכת מרדות הואיל ועשו איסור. ויש לאיש להקפיד
על אשתו בדבר זה ולמנוע הנשים הידועות בכך מליכנס לה ושלא
לצאת היא אליהן.

Tur, Even HaEzer, Laws of Marriage, *Siman* 20

Women who are *mesolelot* one with another - meaning
they connect with one another through intercourse — [it
is] forbidden, and this is *maaseh Eretz Mitzrayim* that we
have been warned about, as it is written, "Do not copy the
practices of the Land of Egypt where you dwelled." And the
Chakhamim, of blessed memory, said, "What would they
do? A man would marry a man, and a woman would marry
a woman, and a woman would be married to two men."
And even though it is forbidden, [the court] does not give
lashes for it, and the woman is not prohibited from [being
with] her husband [because] of this, and it is appropriate
to seclude her and to hit her blows of rebellion, since they
have committed a violation. And a man should be careful
to keep his wife away from this matter. And he should stop
women who are known to engage in this behavior from
coming into his home and keep his wife away from going
out to them.

Before we move to the Shulchan Aruch, let us take a look at the commentary
of Rabbi Yehoshua Falk (Poland, d. 1614) known as the Prisha. He is bothered by the formulation of the Tur, which is a restatement of the Rambam. It
is significant that his approach can be understood as a reading of Rambam
as well. He first points out that the cases of the Sifra can all be viewed as a
kind of rejection of the obligation to be fruitful and multiply. In *Siman* 20
in Even HaEzer (note 11):

פרישה אבן העזר הלכות אישות סימן כ אות יא
(יא) מה היו עושין איש נושא איש כו' ואשה ניסת לשני אנשים. נראה
דרצה לומר דכל מעשיהם שלא לקיים פריה ורביה היו עושים. אך כל
אחד למלאות תאותם שכמו שהאיש הנושא איש, ואשה אשה אינו מו־
ליד כן אשה אחת ניסת לשני אנשים לא לפריה ורביה היו עושים כי מי

שיודע שלא על שמו יקרא הזרע אינו מוליד כמעשה ער ואונן ובודאי
היו משחיתים את זרעם דש מבפנים וזורה מבחוץ לכך נקטינהו בהדדי.

Prisha, Even HaEzer, Laws of Marriage, *Siman* 20:11
"And what would they do? A man would marry a man…
and a woman would be married to two men." It seems that
he wanted to say that they did all their deeds in order to
not fulfill *being fruitful and multiplying*. But they were all to
meet their sexual appetites. For just as when a man marries
a man or woman marries a woman they do not procreate,
likewise one woman who is married to two men, they were
not doing it for the purpose of being fruitful and multiplying, because anyone who knows that the offspring will not
bear his name will not procreate, [he would] behave like
Er and Onen and for sure would spill their seed through
masturbation.

Here the Prisha understands the marriages that are considered *maaseh Eretz
Mitzrayim*, including those of two women, as an attempt to gain sexual gratification without procreating. His assertion is that none of these relationships
intend to build families by having children. All four marriages can almost
be reduced to the prohibition of masturbation like Er and Onan.

His next claim is that the verse from Vayikra, which we originally read as
referring to all four kinds of marriages, is actually only meant to categorize
those relationships that are already *arayot*. In this section, he is treating the
relationship of two women as different from the three others noted in the
Sifra.

והיותר נראה משום דכתב דנשים המסוללות זו בזו אסור דמשמע
איסור בעלמא. וקשה ליה כיון דנפקא מקרא הוה ליה למימר שהוא
דאורייתא? לכך סתם וכתב דיש לומר דהקרא איירי במה שהיו עושין
עוד - שאשה אחת נשאת לשני אנשים דהוא ערוה גמורה לישראל.

And what appears more [logical[to me is that when he
wrote that *nashim hameseolot* are prohibited that it sounds
like a general prohibition. And this is difficult, for if it is
learned from a verse it ought to be a biblical prohibition?
Therefore he wrote simply that verse refers to the other

marriages - a woman marrying two men, because this is a complete *erva* for a Jew.

This approach to the Tur and the Rambam severely limits the prohibition of *maaseh Eretz Mitzrayim* and leaves only the concern of *mesolelot* when dealing with two women.

Rabbi Yosef Karo, in his codification of this law, assumes the Rambam's connection between *nashim mesolelot* and *maaseh Eretz Mitzrayim*. He also understands that *mesolelot* is forbidden as a kind of subset of *maaseh Eretz Mitzrayim*.

שולחן ערוך אבן העזר הלכות אישות סימן כ סעיף ב
(יא) נשים המסוללות (פי' המשחקות ומתחככות) זו בזו, [ז] אסור
ממעשה ארץ מצרים (ויקרא יח:ג) שהוזהרנו עליו. וראוי להכותן מכת
מרדות, הואיל ועשו איסור. ויש לאיש להקפיד על אשתו מדבר זה,
ומונע הנשים הידועות בכך מלהכנס לה ומלצאת היא אליהן.

Shulchan Aruch, Even HaEzer, 20:2
Women who are *mesolelot* (meaning: playing and rubbing) one with another - This is forbidden from *maaseh Eretz Mitzrayim* (Vayikra 18:3) that we have been warned about. And it is appropriate to lash them with whips of rebellion, since they have committed a violation. And a man should be careful to keep his wife away from this matter. And he should stop women who are known to engage in this behavior from coming into his home and keep his wife away from going out to them.

It is significant to simply point out at this stage that for the Shulchan Aruch, as well as the Rambam, the prohibition is stated and placed into the context of a marriage. They advise men to "keep their wives away from" the other women who are known to engage in this kind of behavior.

The Beit Shmuel in his short comment (אות יא) points out that, even though there is a prohibition from engaging in this behavior, doing so does not make this woman unfit to marry a priest. In addition, the Gra (אות ב) quotes the Sifra in full.

These texts demonstrate that two main approaches emerge from the Rishonim and the codes. The minority position is that of the Rambam, who subsumes *nashim mesolelot* under *maaseh Eretz Mitzrayim*. The majority voice among the Rishonim, as represented by Rashi, Tosafot, Ramban, Rashba, Ritva, Ran, and Nimukei Yosef, simply never mentions the Sifra or the Rambam. While it is difficult to prove that all those Rishonim actively reject the Rambam, it does seem clear that they offer an alternative view of the *sugya* that can stand on its own.

II. Analytical Frames

Returning to Rav Huna

A substantial cadre of Acharonim are interested in unpacking the more stringent view of Rav Huna, particularly as understood by Rashi and the Rivan. As they work their way through the Gemara and Rishonim, they build two competing approaches to *mesolelot*: Rambam versus everyone else. What will ultimately emerge from these *mekorot* is an approach that understands *mesolelot* as referring to marital betrayal.

Aruch LaNer (d. 1871, Germany)
Rabbi Yaakov Ettlinger, in his essential commentary on the Talmud, Aruch LaNer, on Yevamot (76a) begins his analysis with the unusual approach of the Rivan that *mesolelot* refers to a woman moving sperm from her husband to another woman. He explains that "certainly the idea of *z'nut* cannot refer to [just] a woman unless it were similar to male intercourse, like when there is the presence of sperm."[36] He goes on to say that perhaps we can understand this Rivan based on the unique position of Rashi that *nashim mesolelot* are forbidden only to the high priest.

The Aruch LaNer notes that Tosafot were bothered by this approach to Rashi, and then he says:

עֲרוּךְ לַנֵר מַסֶּכֶת יבמות דַף עו עַמוּד א, בד״ה הַמְסוֹלֶלֶת
וּבְיוֹתֵר תמוה דרש״י סוֹתֵר דִּבְרֵי עַצְמוֹ דְּהָכָא פִּי׳ מִשּׁוּם זוֹנָה וְהָתָם
מִשּׁוּם בְּעוּלָה

Aruch laNer, Yevamot 76a (commenting on Tosafot, s.v. *Hamesolelot*)
And it is even more of a wonderment as Rashi contradicted his own words. Here [Yevamot] he explained [Rav Huna's

stringency] because of *zona* and there [Shabbat] because
of *be'ula*.

Here he explicitly points out the internal contradiction in Rashi that we
noted above. He then posits that perhaps both Rashi and the Rivan were
bothered by the question of the Rashba (in Shabbat) and the Ritva (in Yevamot)[37] regarding the relationship between Rav Huna and Rebbi Elazar.
The answer that Rav Ettlinger offers is deeply insightful on a human level
and a creative approach to the textual ambiguity at play:

ערוך לנר יבמות דף עו עמוד א
ולכן סבירא להו לרש"י והריב"ן דבאמת לא פסיל רב הונא רק בנ־
שואות דהוי כזנות ממש דפוסל משום דהוי כבא על אשת איש דנפסלה
לכהונה.

Aruch LaNer, Yevamot 76a
Therefore both Rashi and the Rivan think that Rav Huna
did not really declare [*nashim mesolelot*] unfit [for marrying a priest] except in the case of married women, when it
is like real *z'nut*. For then he declared [them] unfit because
it is like a woman who has relations with a married woman
who becomes unfit for the priesthood.

This approach to Rav Huna, that he is talking about a woman married to
a man having an affair with another woman, is difficult to sustain in the
context of the Gemara in Shabbat about Shmuel's father. In that context,
the Gemara at first thought that Rav Huna could be a support to Shmuel's
father — but that case must be one of unmarried women. The *Aruch LaNer*
explains that this is indeed a problem according to the הו"א (what the Gemara may have originally thought), but that it makes perfect sense according
to the conclusion that, in fact, Rav Huna cannot be seen as a support to
Shmuel's father:

ערוך לנר מסכת יבמות דף עו עמוד א
אבל לפי מה דמסיק דלא משום דרב הונא הוי שפיר מסקינן דטעמא
משום זונה דאשת איש ולא שייך רק בנשואות או משום מטילות ש"ז
דלא שייך ג"כ רק בנשואות

---

[37] As well as the Ramban in Shabbat, as noted above, see footnote 30 for a brief description of the
question.

Aruch LaNer, Yevamot 76a
But according to the conclusion [of the Gemara in Shabbat]
that [Shmuel's father was not stringent because of] Rav
Huna, it is appropriate to conclude that it was because of
zona like a married woman, which only applies to wom-
en who are married or because they are sharing semen —
which also only applies to married women.

The claim of the Aruch LaNer is that Rav Huna's opposition to *mesolelot* is
based on the assumption that at least one of these women is married to a
man and basically having an affair. While this relationship may not technically be adultery because we are only talking about two women and, in the
Aruch LaNer's framework, there is no such thing as intercourse without the
presence of a man, this woman has nonetheless violated the *kedusha* of her
marriage. Rav Huna therefore goes so far as to say that this kind of marital
betrayal makes a woman unfit to marry a priest.

Rava, however, rejects Rav Huna's claim and says that since we are, at the
end of the day, talking about a case that can never be considered intercourse,
this ought to be considered "mere licentiousness."[38] If both Rav Huna AND
Rava are talking about a woman who is married to a man and is having an
affair with another woman, then it turns out that the Gemara says absolutely
nothing about two single women engaging in intimate physical behavior.

Rabbi Yaakov Ettlinger is reading the two *sugyot* about *mesolelot* (Shabbat
65a and Yevamot 76a) according to Rashi, Rivan, Ramban, Rashba, and
Ritva and at no point makes mention of Rambam or *maaseh Eretz Mitzrayim*. His creative reading comes from a question that bothered many of
these Rishonim, and he solves the problem with a single insight: that one
of the women has to be married to a man for the opinion of Rav Huna (or
perhaps even Rava) to apply.

Ishei Yisrael (d. 1889, Slotzk)
A similar idea appears in the commentary of Rabbi Yisrael Isser ben Mordechai Isserlein. He writes in his commentary on Shabbat 65a,[39] אשי ישראל,
as follows:

---

[38] The Aruch LaNer answers the textual question as well in the following manner:
והא דקאמר "ואפילו לרבי אלעזר דאמר פנוי הבא על הפנויה עשאה זונה" לא משום דטעם דרב הונא כרבי אלעזר אלא דהכי
קאמר - דליתא לדרב הונא דודאי לא חשיב זה זנות אשת איש. ואפילו לרבי אלעזר דפנויה נעשית זונה ולא בעי זונה כשמה
שזונה מתחת בעלה, אפילו הכי מודה בזה, דזה לא הוי רק פריצותא בעלמא.
[39] See page לו in the Vilna ed., 1864. At the end of the introduction he claims to be a descendant of the
Rema.

אשי ישראל חלק ראשון מסכת שבת דף ס"ה ע"א
ולולא דמיסתפינא הייתי אומר דרב הונא לא מיירי כלל בדין פנויה
אלא באשת איש.
ועריות בבנתיה דשמואל, דאלו ע"י זכר היו חייבין כרת.
ואשמעינן דלכהונה אין נפ"מ בין זכר לנקבה.

Ishei Yisrael, Shabbat 65a

And if I were not afraid I would say that Rav Huna was not
at all dealing with the law regarding a single woman, but
rather only regarding a married woman and *arayot*. And
regarding the daughters of Shmuel['s father] he was talking
about a case in which if the paramour had been a man they
would have been liable for divine excision. And we learn
that regarding [the permission to marry into the] priesthood there is no difference between a man and a woman.

Here he addresses the Gemara about Shmuel's sisters by adding that *mesolelot* could be thought of as problematic if one of the women is married
to a man or if the two women are related to each other in such a way that
if one of them were a man it would be a relationship prohibited by *karet*.
He goes on to refer to this very approach within the Aruch LaNer as well.

Kiryat Melech Rav (d. 1844, Jerusalem) on the שחוף (shachuf)[40]

Rav Yehuda ben Efraim Navon, who was born in Jerusalem and eventually
served as the chief rabbi of the holy city, was an important Sefaradi *posek*.
He was asked to address a complicated question regarding a married man
whom he categorizes as a *shachuf*, who had an affair with another woman.
This question touches on many different areas of *halakha*. Here is the way
this man is introduced:

מעשה שהיה בעירנו באיש שהוא בן תורה שמוחזק אצלנו בבירור שאין
לו גבורת אנשים כלל ונשען על ביתו ולא יעמוד וכשבא באיזה זמן על
אשתו בדוחק משמש באבר מת כמ"ש הר"מ ז"ל ויהי היום ונתפס האיש
ההוא שחבק ונשק ערוה אחת ומנהגינו לענש נכסין על הקריבות והוא

---

[40] See Bavli Sotah 26b and Shavuot 18a for the Gemara's brief treatment of the case of the *shachuf* and
sex with a flaccid organ. See also Rambam Hil. Issurei Biah 1:11, Tur Even HaEzer 20:1 (it is interesting
that the same סימן in the Tur deals with both this issue as well as *mesolelot*), *Beit Yosef* 185. See also the
פרי האדמה on the Rambam Hil. Issurei Biah 1:11, who deals at length with the same kind of question.
In addition, in the סימן י"ט (there appear to be two ספר נחפה בכסף ח"ב אב"ע סימן י"ט's in this volume, and
it is the first one).

אמוד וכשרצה להענישו טען שלגבי דידיה אין זה איסור וטעמו שדברי
הר"מ ז"ל בזה נראה שעיקר איסור הקריבות הוי מפני הרגל עבירה
שמא יבא עליה ובדידיה אפי' אם יבא ליכא איסור תורה

There was the following case in our city of a man who is a
ben-Torah and knows with certainty to us that he does not
at all have the male power [to procreate], and he "rests on
his house and cannot stand."[41] And when he had relations
with his wife with difficulty, he did so with a flaccid organ,
as the Rambam (Hil. Issurei Biah 1:11) says. And behold
one day this man was caught having hugged and kissed
an *erva*. And the practice in our city is to give a monetary
fine for this kind of behavior - and he has been evaluated
for this purpose. And when [we] went to punish him, he
claimed that for him there is no prohibition according to
the Rambam. It seems that the essence of the prohibition
of "coming close" [to an *erva*] is because it can lead to more
regular sinning, lest it lead to intercourse — and with him,
even if he were to have relations with her there is no Torah
prohibition.

Rabbi Navon brings up the topic of *mesolelot* as a potential analogy to his
case in an attempt to adjudicate this question. He begins his analysis as
follows:

והייתי רוצה להביא ראיה שיש איסור תורה בזה דרך דמיון, והוא דלא
גרע זה מאשה, והדין הוא דנשים המסוללות אסור...דכך נוטה הסברא
דהשתא אשה עם אשה אסר רחמנא זה השחוף עם העריות אינו דין
שיאסר רחמנא?

And I wanted to bring proof that there is a Torah prohibition of a [*shachuf*] in this regard from an analogy. And that
is that [the *shachuf*] is no less than a woman, and the law is
that *nashim hamesolelot* is forbidden... This is where the
logic leans, for if the Torah forbade a woman from having
relations with another woman, this *shachuf* with one of the
arayot, would the law not be to forbid him?

---

[41] A euphemism for the inability to have an erection.

In the middle of this section he quotes the Rambam and takes for granted that there is a Torah prohibition of *mesolelot*. Given that starting point, obviously a *shachuf* should be at least as forbidden to have relations with a woman as two women would be with each other. However, Rav Navon then goes back to the Bavli with Rashi and Tosafot and understands that the simple reading of the *sugyot* does not accord with Rambam:

ובהיותי ע"ז נתקשתי דמסוגיין דשבת הנזכר נראה דליכא איסור תורה כי האי גוונא.

And when I was in this matter I was bothered, because from the *sugya* in Shabbat it appears that there is no Torah prohibition in this manner [two women].

He then quotes the Gemara with Rashi and says:

משמע דאין בדבר זה אפילו איסור דרבנן אלא דמכוער הדבר.

And it sounds like in this matter there is not even a rabbinic prohibition, rather it is disgusting.

Rav Navon claims that, according to Rashi and the conclusion of the Bavli, there is no formal prohibition associated with *mesolelot;* it is just "מכוער — disgusting." This is how he understands Rashi's comment on "mere licentiousness." He goes on to reject the Rambam's conflation from within the Gemara itself:

וכן מוכח מהסוגיא, דאל"כ ל"ל דרב הונא תיפוק ליה דהיה נזהר שמואל בזה משום לאו דכמעשה ארץ מצרים. וכן מוכח ג"כ ממאי דדחי תל־מודא, "לא, סבר כי היכי דלא לילפן ופי' רש"י ז"ל דלא לילפן גופא נוכראה והתאוו לשכב עם איש" ע"כ. ואם איתא דאיכא איסור תורה במסוללות או אפי' איסור דרבנן תיפוק ליה משום שלא יהיו מסוללות. מכח קושיא זו הייתי רוצה לומר דהאמת כמ"ש ריב"ן וכל מסוללות כדרך שכתב ריב"ן אז יש איסור תורה אבל כל כי ההיא דשמואל שהיו בתולות אפ' אסורא ליכא אלא כי היכי דלא לילפן.

And so it must be, according to the *sugya*. For if this were not the case, why would the Gemara quote Rav Huna as a support to Shmuel's [father's] being cautious about this? The *sugya* should quote the prohibition of *maaseh Eretz Mitzrayim*. And it also must be based on the Talmud's rejection, "No, he did not want them to become accustomed to a foreign body." And Rashi explained, "And they would desire to sleep with a man." And if it were true that there is a Torah prohibition of *mesolelot*, or even a rabbinic prohibition, they should have explained [Shmuel's father's stringency as being so that] they [the daughters] would not be *mesolelot*. From the strength of this question, I would want to say that the truth accords with the Rivan and that women who are *mesolelot* in the way the Rivan said would have violated a Torah prohibition. However, if it were like the case of Shmuel['s father's daughters], who were unmarried, there is not even a prohibition except "not becoming accustomed."

Rabbi Navon says that if two women were to engage in the *mesolelot* as described by the Rivan, sharing their husbands' sperm, such behavior would be a Torah prohibition. This limiting of the definition of *mesolelot* is supported by the fact that Shmuel's father was not concerned about it, as a *maaseh Eretz Mitzrayim* or some technical prohibition of physical intimacy between two women. If he had been, the Gemara would have used that to explain his stringency.

Rav Navon goes on to say:

אמנם עדיין קשה על הרמז"ל דמסתמיות דבריו נראה דאפי' בפנויות איכא איסור תורה. וכן ק' על התוס' שדחו פי' ריב"ן, ולפי דבריהם נראה דמסוללות ליכא איסר אפי' מדרבנן כאמור.

However, it is still difficult regarding the Rambam, *z"l*, because from the simple reading of his words, it appears that even with single women there is a Torah prohibition. And it is also difficult regarding Tosafot, who rejected the explanation of the Rivan. For according to their [Tosafot's] words, there is not even a rabbinic prohibition, as has been said.

According to the Rivan and Tosafot, there is simply no prohibition of *mesolelot* without the sharing of semen between two women.

אך עדיין קשה עליהם אמאי לא הקשו עליו מברייתא דתורת כהנים?
דמשם מוכח דאיכא איסור. דמסוגיין דסנהדרין [צ"ל שבת] משמע
דליכא איסורא. וגם דברי הרמז"ל עדיין קשים דהוא ס"ל דאיכא איסור
תורה אפילו בפנויה והתם משמע דליכא איסור כלל.

But there is still a question about them [those who hold
there is fundamentally no prohibition]: why didn't they
[the Gemara] ask on him from the *baraita* [in the *Sifra*]
about the laws of priests - because from there it is clear that
there is a prohibition. Because from the *sugya* in Sanhedrin
[should read: Shabbat] it appears that there is no prohibition. And also the words of the Rambam, *z"l*, are still
difficult because he thinks that there is a Torah prohibition
even with a single woman and there [Shabbat] it sounds
like there is no prohibition at all.

Here Rabbi Navon asks a very sharp question. If indeed *maaseh Eretz Mitzrayim* stands alone as a separate prohibition, as the Rambam said, why didn't
the Gemara quote the Sifra to explain Shmuel's father's stringency regarding
his daughters? It seems clear that the Bavli, together with Rashi, Rivan,
and Tosafot, does not accept the Sifra. Therefore, Rabbi Navon devises a
creative way to read the Rambam: that there can only be a prohibition of
the two women actually getting married and living "דרך אישות — in the way
of marriage."[42]

Rabbi Navon is not even sure that this answer can be sustained within
the Rambam, "כי עשו דרך נישואין מאי הוי... אין זה כי אם שיחת נשים — because if
they were doing something akin to marriage, what would it be... it would be
nothing but women's conversation." He ultimately tries to force this reading
into the Rambam but concludes that, according to Rashi (and the majority
of Rishonim), there is simply no prohibition.

Dibrot Moshe, Rav Moshe Feinstein (d. 1986, New York City)
Rav Moshe Feinstein, in the second volume of the Dibrot Moshe on Shabbat
סימן נג הערה לה[43], assumes that there it at least a rabbinic prohibition accord-

---

[42] Rav Eldad Sabag in his באר המלך on the Rambam Hil. Issurei Biah 21:8 אות קסט page ת offers a similar
idea that with an actual marriage there could be a Torah prohibition, "ובזה יש מן גרשפנקא לעצם המעשה."
[43] This volume of the Dibrot was originally published in 1976 and then subsequently reprinted, together with Volume One, by the Mesorah Heritage Foundation in 1996 to mark the 10th *yahrtzeit* of Rav
Moshe. It is interesting to note that in February of 1976, the same year that this short essay on *nashim
mesolelot* was published, Rav Moshe also published his *teshuva* about homosexual men. See Igrot Moshe

ing to Rambam and that there may even be a Torah prohibition as well. He
begins his analysis by asking a series of strong questions against Rav Huna.[44]
His attempt to explain Rav Huna concludes with the following supposition:

ואולי משום זה פרש"י שהוא לכ"ג

And maybe because of this [Rav Moshe's own questions]
Rashi claimed that it [the prohibition is only against mar-
riage] to the high priest.

As I pointed out above, there is an apparent contradiction within Rashi's
approach to Rav Huna. Here, Rav Moshe is using the more stringent reading within Rashi to help understand why Rav Huna would even claim that
women who are *mesolelot* are unfit to marry the high priest. Rav Moshe
continues:

דברור דנשים כאלו הן מצד רצונם ותאותם הגדולה יש להן תאוה
גדולה גם לזנות אם יזדמן להן ושייך לחושדן מצד תאותן... מ"מ סובר
ר"ה שלכ"ג אסרוה מדרבנן לגודל קדושתו שהקפידה עליו תורה מלישא
אישה שנבעלה אף בעילת היתר שלכן החמירו עליו מדרבנן לפסול
עליו אישה שתאותה גדולה לזנות אף שלא אסרו אותה לכהן הדיוט
משום שעכ"פ אינה זונה.

For it is clear that women like this [*mesolelot*] from their
strong sexual desire they must also have a great desire for
z'nut [with men] if it were made available to them. Therefore, it is appropriate to suspect them because of their desire… Nonetheless Rav Huna thinks that there is a Rabbinic prohibition to marry the high priest because of the
greatness of his holiness. For the Torah was stringent about

<hr />

Orach Chaim 4 #115, where his language of disgust regarding gay men takes on a very different tone
than his language regarding women. Some of the polemic in opposition to male homosexual sex can
be understood as emerging from the Biblical text. However, in both pieces, Rav Moshe simply does not
understand the phenomenon of same-sex attraction. In many ways, Rav Moshe was a product of his
time in this regard. Thank God, we have a different awareness in the 21st century.
[44] Rav Moshe quotes three different Gemarot that pose a problem for Rav Huna. First, he refers to
Yevamot 55a, which talks about the definition of intercourse and assumes penetration of some kind.
Second, he quotes Yevamot 59a, which explains that if a woman committed bestiality, she would not
be prohibited from marrying a priest. Finally, he brings Ketubot 36b about a non-Jewish captor who
may have rubbed his genitals against his Jewish captive's body and nonetheless does not make her unfit
for a priest.

his not marrying even a woman who had permissible sex; therefore [the ruling of Rav Huna] was stringent on him rabbinically, [determining that] a woman with a great desire for *z'nut* is unfit [to marry him] even though she is not [considered] unfit for a simple priest because nevertheless she is not a *zona.*

Rav Moshe here makes a bold claim that the reason Rav Huna forbade these women from marrying the high priest was not their intimate behavior with each other per se but that such actions reflect uncontrollable sexual desire. The unique nature of the high priest is that he is not allowed to marry a woman who has engaged even in permissible intercourse with a man (e.g., a widow). Given that special status, Rav Moshe claims that a woman with an overactive libido is prohibited from marrying the high priest.

Although Rav Moshe ultimately concludes in accordance with Rambam that being *nashim mesolelot* is forbidden, his creative reading of Rav Huna forces him to analyze the fact that, at least according to the Bavli, there really is no prohibition on the physical act of intimacy between two women. The only concern is what it might lead to at some future stage. Like Shmuel's father, who was worried that if his daughters shared a bed they would grow used to sleeping with another body and then be drawn to men in an inappropriate fashion, so too Rav Moshe explains Rav Huna's stringency.

Only after his analysis of Rav Huna does Rav Moshe raise the concept of *maaseh Eretz Mitzrayim.* He refers to the Rambam's combination of the two ideas and, at first, thinks that *maaseh Eretz Mitzrayim* ought to be a Torah prohibition. However, Rav Moshe goes on to explain that, with two women, it is simply not possible to ever reach the level of a Torah prohibition because, even for the Rambam, the Torah prohibition is only possible with two people who are considered by the Torah in danger of having relations that are *arayot.*

שזה לא שייך בנשים המסוללות ששום דבר מהקריבות לא שייך שיביאו
לידי גילוי ערוה שהוא ביאה, שלכן א"א בשום אופן לומר שאיכא לאו
מן התורה בזה... והיא כוונת הרמב"ם שליכא מלקות אף אם הוא
מדאורייתא משום שאין לו לאו מיוחד ועוד שגם לאו ממש מדאורייתא
ליכא דהרי אין שם ביאה כלל...

For this would not be relevant in the context of *nashim hamesolelot* because none of their intimate physical behaviors is related to leading to *giluy erva* [a Torah prohibition], which is intercourse. Therefore it is impossible under any circumstances to say that there is a Torah prohibition... And the intention of the Rambam who says that there are no *malkot* even if it were to be a Torah prohibition because it has no specific prohibition. And also because there is no real Torah prohibition because there is no intercourse at all.

Rav Moshe in this section makes it clear that, even according to Rambam, there cannot possibly be a Torah prohibition because there is no possibility of fulfilling the *halakhic* definition of sex.

Rav Moshe then goes on to explain the Gemara in Shabbat 65a/b in the following creative fashion:

והיה שייך לפרש דהלימא מסייע הוא רק לענין האיסור ואמר מסייע לו לר"ה משום שלא הוזכר גם עצם האיסור מאמוראי אחריני, ואף שהיא ברייתא בתו"כ... ונקט גם זה דאשה נושאת אשה דזה ודאי אינו דבר איסור לבני נח וגם לא מצינו שהוא איסור לישראל. שלכן היה מקום לומר דלא נקט דוקא מילי דאיסורי אלא כל הדברים שנעשים רק לתאוה יתירה מדרך העולם שבאים מזה לעשות מעשה הגדולים והמתועבים...

And it would have been appropriate to explain the Gemara's "it should be supported" as referring only to the prohibition. And it said "it should be supported by Rav Huna" because this prohibition itself is not mentioned by any other Amoraim, even though there is a *baraita* in the laws of priests [the Sifra]... And [the Sifra] referred to a woman marrying a woman, which certainly is not prohibited for the Noachides and we have not found that it is prohibited for the Jews. And therefore there is room to say that it [the Sifra] did not only refer to relationships that are prohibited, rather all matters that are done because of excessive lust that in the way of the world that leads people to commit abominable acts.

Here Rav Moshe is making three important points. First, he notes that no other Amoraim say anything in support of Rav Huna. Second, although he does not ask the question explicitly, he is clearly bothered by the fact that the Gemara in Shabbat does not refer to the Sifra in support of Shmuel's father's stringency regarding his daughters. And, finally, here he repeats that there really is no formal prohibition against women engaging in sexual intimacy but rather *mesolelot* reflects an overdeveloped libido that is not easy to control.

He concludes his brief essay with the following question:

אבל הא ברש"י מפורש דהמקשה היה סבור דכל הקפידא דהיה שייך
להקפיד לאבוה דשמואל הוא רק מחמת סובר כר"ה דפסול לכהונה
גדולה ולתוס' גם לכהן הדיוט, שזה תמוה דודאי בשביל איסור אף
אם רק מדרבנן יש להקפיד שלא יבוא לידי כך וכ"ש אם הוא איסורא
דאורייתא אף שהם כשרות לכהונה, וצע"ג.

But here in Rashi it is clear that the questioner [original-ly] thought that the entire stringency that Shmuel's father deemed necessary was only because he held like Rav Huna who [considered *nashim mesolelot*] unfit for [marrying] the high priest, and for Tosafot also for a simple priest, and this is a wonderment! For certainly because of a prohibition, even if it were only rabbinic, it is appropriate to be stringent in making sure it does not come to happen, all the more so if there were a Torah prohibition, even if they were to still be considered fit to [marry into] the priesthood. And this requires great further analysis.

Rav Moshe here is asking a very simple question: if there is a known rabbinic (all the more so, Torah) prohibition that is learned in the Sifra, why doesn't the Gemara give that as the explanation for Shmuel's father not permitting his daughters to share a bed?[45] According to Rashi and Tosafot's reading, we might conclude that, since we *pasken* like Rava against Rav Huna (and like Beit Hillel against Beit Shammai), and *nashim mesolelot* remain permitted to a priest, there may in fact be no prohibition!

Rav Moshe says that we must therefore say that, according to Rashi and Tosafot, there cannot possibly be a Torah prohibition. It is even difficult to claim that this is a rabbinic prohibition. He concludes as follows:

---

[45] Here Rav Moshe is dealing with Rashi and Tosafot; below I will address the Bavli on its own terms.

...ואולי לגמרי רק מדרנן, שלכן היה סבור המקשה דרק אם סובר כר"ה
דהוא גם פסול לכהונה שאם תנשא לכהן יהיה מכשול לאחרים חשש
ביותר וגם בשביל מעלה לכהונה. אבל זה שייך רק לתוס' דגם לכהן
הדיוט פוסל ר"ה, אבל לרש"י שרק לכ"ג פסול הרי לא יהיה מזה מכ־
שול עדיין יקשה, ואולי בשביל לעז דשם זנות החמיר יותר ועדיין צ"ע.

And perhaps it is entirely a rabbinic [prohibition], and that
therefore the questioner thought that only if Shmuel's father
thought like Rav Huna that she is unfit to marry into the
priesthood, for he was exceedingly concerned that if she
were to marry a priest it might be a stumbling block for
others and also because of a higher [level of purity associat-
ed] with the priesthood. But this is only relevant according
to Tosafot, who understand that Rav Huna rules that she is
is unfit even for a simple priest, but according to Rashi,
who prohibits her only to the high priest, there is no future
stumbling block, the matter is still difficult. And perhaps
because of the bad name of *z'nut* he was extra stringent.
And the matter requires further analysis.

The above material is all addressing only Rashi and Tosafot, whose views
made it hard for Rav Moshe to identify a prohibition. Again, it is important
to make this point clear. Rav Moshe understands that the Bavli by itself does
not prohibit intimate sexual behavior between two women. For Rashi and
Tosafot (and nearly everyone besides Rambam), who do not quote the Sifra,
that is the conclusion of the *sugya*. What the Gemara says implicitly, Rav
Moshe says explicitly: without *maaseh Eretz Mitzrayim* (and the Rambam),
there really is no prohibition of *nashim mesolelot*.

I conclude my analysis of Rav Moshe with a short excerpt from one of
his many *teshuvot* in support of Artificial Insemination by Donor (AID).[46]
The Rivan's understanding of the concept of *nashim mesolelot* appears to be
a version of some kind of transfer of semen from a man to a woman other
than his wife. Rav Moshe was the champion of the cause of AID against
many other *poskim*.[47] In his letter to Rav Breisch, at the very end of אב"ע
סימן כא of the חלקת יעקב, Rav Moshe writes:

---

[46] See Igrot Moshe Even HaEzer volume 1 *teshuvot* 10, 11, and 71 for Rav Moshe's strong support of
AID, to which many were vehemently opposed.

[47] When Rabbi Mordechai Yaakov Breisch (b. Poland 1896) fled to Switzerland in 1934, he carried on
correspondence with many *gedolim*. The opening *teshuvot* in his Even HaEzer all deal with a similar

טו) ומצד איסור נשים המסוללות, אף אם נימא כפירוש הריב"ן דמטי-
לות ש"ז שקבלו מבעליהן, פשוט שכיון שהאיסור הוא פריצותא, הוא
רק כשהוא לתכלית פריצות, כהא דמעשה ארצ"מ אשה נושא אשה
ואיש נושא איש, ולא כשעושין זה להוליד ולד, שלא שייך לאסור מצד
פריצות כיון שאינו לכוונת פריצות כלל ולא לשם תאווה...

And from the perspective of the prohibition of *nashim
hamesolelot*, even if we say like the explanation of the Rivan
that they are placing semen that they received from their
husbands [into the other woman] it is clear that since the
prohibition is *pritzuta*, it is only prohibited when it is for a
licentious goal similar to *maaseh eretz Mitzrayim* - when a
woman marries a woman or a man marries a man — and
not when they engage in this behavior in order to procreate.
It is not appropriate to forbid because of licentiousness
since this is not for a licentious purpose, and not for the
sake of lust...

Rav Moshe's claim here is that even if you understand *mesolelot* like the
Rivan, and it turns out that the Gemara was actually referring to a kind of
artificial insemination, that would not apply to the contemporary circumstances of a couple struggling with infertility. The implication of this sentence is radical: כיון שהאיסור הוא פריצותא, הוא רק כשהוא לתכלית פריצות — since
the prohibition [of *mesolelot*] is because of licentiousness, it is only when
done for a licentious purpose." One simply cannot refer to a married couple
seeking to build a family as *pritzut*; if anything, it is exactly the opposite.

Rav Breisch, despite the fact that he published this letter in his own *sefer*,
was shocked by this paragraph by Rav Moshe. He understood that the implications of Rav Moshe's claim could indeed be very extreme. He begins by
quoting the Gemara, Rambam, and Magid Mishneh and then says:

שו"ת חלקת יעקב הערות לאבן העזר סימן כא הערה ג
ג) /הערת המחבר/...אם כן הגע בעצמך הכי יעלה על הדעת שאם נשים
יעשו מעשה נבלה מסוללות לאיזה תכלית ממון, שרופא אחד נתן להם
ממון לעשות זאת בכדי ללמוד איזה מדע מזה, וכדומה שיש למצא איזו
משכחת שהנשים עושין זאת לא לשם תאווה רק לאיזה תכלית אחר,
הכי יעלה על הדעת שמותר לעבור על לאו הכתוב בתורה בשביל תכ-

---

set of issues of complex parentage. He has several letters back and forth with Rav Moshe about artificial
insemination by donor.

לית או כיו"ב, דברים כאלו מביאים לידי גיחוך, וכת"ה בסברא בעלמא
"כיון שאינו לכוונת פריצות כלל ולא לשם תאוה" מתיר איסור תורה
המבואר ברמב"ם וברה"מ...

Chelkat Yaakov, notes to Even HaEzer, *Siman* 21 note #3
...If so, look carefully yourself, how could one even consider
that if women would engage in *mesolelot*, this disgusting
behavior, for some financial purpose — that a doctor [were
conducting a study and] was paying them to do this in order to gain scientific knowledge, or the like — and we could
find a rationale [to believe] that the women were doing this
not because of lust, but for some other purpose, how could
one even consider that it is permissible to violate a negative
commandment written in the Torah merely for some other
purpose or something similar. This type of thinking leads
to absurdity and laughter. And how could you, based on
your own logical thinking that "since it is not for a licentious intention at all and not for the sake of desire" permit
a Torah prohibition that is elaborated on in the Rambam
and the Magid Mishneh?

To be clear, Rav Moshe is not prepared to overlook the Rambam and still assumes that *maaseh Eretz Mitzrayim* would ultimately be *parutz* (licentious).
However, that concern is only true within the framework of the Rambam
and the Shulchan Aruch. Within Rav Moshe's framework, according to
Rashi and Tosafot (and *rov* Rishonim), there is no technical prohibition of
mesolelot when done in a modest setting. Let us now turn to a contemporary
posek who was (almost) prepared to apply this idea in a live case.

Vaya'an David, Rabbi Chaim Dovid Yosef Weiss, Antwerp (*shlita*)[48]
In the seventh volume of his writings, Rav Weiss has a short essay entitled
"אם מותר לאשה לגרום לעצמה הרגשה — May a woman cause herself to have a
feeling [of sexual pleasure]." He begins his analysis of this question with the
issue of *mesolelot*. First he refers to the two key Gemarot; then he quotes
the Shulchan Aruch and then says:

---

[48] Thank you very much to Rabbi Ysoscher Katz for bringing this fascinating source to my attention.

ולכאורה משמע אפילו ביד. אך ברש"י ותוס' לא משמע כן. וכן כתב
בספר הלבושים דמיירי בשפשוף עריות. אלא דסוף כל סוף לכולי עלמא
הוי מילי דפריצותא. ואין להתיר זאת אפילו בשעת דחק גדול ממש.

And presumably it sounds like this ought to be forbidden
even if done (only) by hand. But according to Rashi and
Tosafot it does not appear that way. And it is also written
in Levush that we are dealing with rubbing of genitals. But
nevertheless ultimately, according to all, this is a matter of
pritzut. And this should not be permitted even in a case of
really great need.

Rav Weiss understands that there is a basic debate between Rashi and Tosafot on one side and the Shulchan Aruch on the other. He points out that even
according to Rashi and Tosafot, who limit *mesolelot* to genital-on-genital
contact (or the exchange of semen), there would still remain the concern
for *pritzuta* (licentiousness). He then makes it clear that even in a case of
"really great need" this could never be permitted. The bulk of the entry then
goes on to address the question of women and masturbation.

The concluding paragraph of this essay offers a surprising question. His
answer represents, to my mind, an application of the position of the majority of Rishonim as filtered through these key Achronim. We will see that
he makes no mention of Rambam, though he quotes the Shulchan Aruch
in full. He presents the position of Rashi and Tosafot — and I would add
Ramban, Rashba, Ritva, Ran, and Nimukei Yosef — in opposition to the
Shulchan Aruch as a simple foil. He writes:

ויען דוד חלק ז אבן העזר (סוף) סימן יג אות ו (עמ' כו, נדפס תשע"א)
עוד נשאלתי מאשה אשר בעלה פורש ממנה, וכדי שתנוח דעתה מן
התאוה, חברתה מפשפשת לה בא"מ [באותו מקום], אם זה אסור? והנה
המחבר (בס' כ') כתב וז"ל, נשים המסוללות אסור ממעשה ארץ מצרים
שהוזהרנו עליו וראוי להכותן מכת מרדות הואיל ועשו איסור, ויש
לאיש להקפיד על אשתו מדבר זה ומונע הנשים הידועות בכך מלהכנס
לה ומלצאת היא אליהן ע"כ. ובהגה על המסוללות כתב המש' ומתח'
זו בזו. ולכאורה משמע אפילו ביד. אך ברש"י ותוס' לא משמע כן. וכן
כתב בספר הלבושים דמיירי בשפשוף עריות. אלא דסוף כל סוף הוי
מילי דפריצותא. ובודאי יש להוכיח בתוכחה עצומה על שבעלה עובר
על מצות עשה דועונתה לא יגרע. ועכ"פ אין להתיר זאת אלא בשעת

דחק גדול ממש, ורק באופן צנוע על ידי אשה צנועה וכנ"ל, ולמעשה
לא התרתי כלל.

Rabbi Chaim Dovid Yosef Weiss, Satmar Dayan in Antwerp, Vaya'an David vol. 7 Siman 13, Section 6 (page 26) - published 5771 (2010/1)

I was also asked by a woman whose husband will not have sex with her, and in order to calm her desire, a friend of hers rubs her privates — is this forbidden?

For behold, the Shulchan Aruch says, "Women who are *mesolelot* one with another — This is forbidden from *maaseh Eretz Mitzrayim* (Vayikra 18:3) that we have been warned about. And it is appropriate to lash them with whips of rebellion, since they have committed a violation. And a man should be careful to keep his wife away from this matter. And he should stop women who are known to engage in this behavior from coming into his home and keep his wife away from going out to them." And presumably it sounds like this ought to be forbidden even if done (only) by hand. But according to Rashi and Tosafot, it does not appear that way. And it is also written in Levush that we are dealing with rubbing of genitals. But nevertheless this is a matter of *pritzut*. And certainly we should rebuke the husband with a strong rebuke for not fulfilling the mitzvah of *onah*. And nevertheless, this should not be permitted except in a case of really great need, and it should only be permitted in a humble fashion with a humble woman. And practically I did not permit it at all.

Note the subtle shift from the opening paragraph to the concluding paragraph. In reference to the *pritzut* associated with *mesolelot*, he begins by saying:

ואין להתיר זאת אפילו בשעת דחק גדול ממש.

And this should not be permitted even in the case of really great need.

However, once there was a serious human (physical) need expressed, he says:

אין להתיר זאת אלא בשעת דחק גדול ממש, ורק באופן צנוע על ידי
אשה צנועה

> this should not be permitted except in a case of really great need, and it should only be permitted in a humble fashion with a humble woman

It is important to note that he was not willing to offer this *psak* on a practical basis and permit this behavior, even though he clearly thinks that it ought technically to be permitted. What is it that theoretically pushed Rav Weiss to entertain the notion that *mesolelot* can be permitted in certain situations? While he does not fully articulate all of the moving parts of his argumentation, it seems clear that he took the following steps:

1. This physical behavior may not even be part of the category of *mesolelot*.
2. *Mesolelot* must be considered a rabbinic violation at most.
3. The key concern is one of modesty and licentiousness.
4. He understands the need for sexual fulfillment to be significant within the *halakhic* process.
5. Within a context of modesty and great need, we can permit what might otherwise be viewed as a violation of rabbinic notions of *pritzut*.

Summary of these Achronim:

I am well aware that this selection of Achronim — from the Aruch LaNer in the 19th century to Rav Weiss in the 21st century — represents only one approach to the question of *mesolelot*. These *poskim* form a substantive position that is formidable and cannot simply be rejected out of hand. While it is impossible to rank the relative standing or authority of groups of rabbis, it is significant that we are talking about *gedolim* the likes of Rav Yaakov Ettlinger and Rav Moshe Feinstein.

This entire group is bothered by a series of shared questions:

1. How can we understand Rav Huna's very extreme position that claims that *nashim mesolelot* are unfit to marry into the priesthood?
2. What do we do with the apparent contradiction in Rashi — all priests or only the high priest?
3. Why does the Rivan explain *mesolelot* as a kind of artificial insemination?

When taken in the aggregate, these Achronim help to solidify my claim that the Rambam is a minority position and that most Rishonim either reject or simply ignore his approach. There may be other ways to answer these questions, but here I claim that, given this cluster of *poskim*, my reading of the Rishonim and the Bavli can stand.

B. Understanding the Bavli on Its Own

Pritzuta b'alma

The Bavli describes the behavior of *nashim mesolelot* as פריצותא בעלמא — mere licentiousness. The *halakhic* system certainly discourages people from engaging in something that is the opposite of צניעות (modesty), but there is a difference between *pritzut* and *issur* (prohibition). In this context, what the Gemara means is that this particular act of physical intimacy between two women is not considered *halakhically* significant enough to prohibit a woman from marrying a priest.

However, one might wonder what the Bavli means when it uses the term פריצותא בעלמא more broadly. Where else does it appear, and what are its implications in those settings?

There are two other *sugyot* that use this phrase. In Masechet Sotah, the Gemara is trying to establish which kinds of behaviors a husband has the right to warn his wife against, such that if she violates them she would be required to undergo the *sotah* ceremony. In this context, the phrase פריצותא בעלמא (mere licentiousness) clearly refers to a prohibited kind of sexual behavior.

תלמוד בבלי מסכת סוטה דף כו עמוד ב
מאי דבר אחר? אמר רב ששת פרט לשקינא לה שלא כדרכה.
אמר ליה רבא שלא כדרכה משכבי אשה כתיב
אלא אמר רבא פרט לשקינא לה דרך אברים
א״ל אביי פריצותא בעלמא היא ופריצותא מי אסר רחמנא

Bavli Sotah 26b (see also Yevamot 55a)

The Gemara asks: **What is** meant by the term: **Something else? Rav Sheshet said:** This **excludes** a case **where** the husband **issued a warning to** his wife not to engage in sexual intercourse **in an atypical manner,** i.e., anal intercourse, with another man, and teaches that this is not considered a valid warning. **Rava said to** Rav Sheshet: Intercourse **in an atypical manner** is considered sexual intercourse, as **it is written: "The cohabitations of a woman" (Leviticus 18:22**), indicating that there are two forms of sexual intercourse with a woman, vaginal and anal, and there is no halakhic differentiation between them. **Rather, Rava said:** It **excludes** a case **where** the husband **issued a warning to** his wife not to engage in intimate contact with another man **by way of** other **limbs,** as this is not considered sexual intercourse. **Abaye said to** Rava: That **is merely licentious** behavior, **and does the Merciful One render** a woman **forbidden** to her husband on account of merely **licentious** behavior, without sexual intercourse? Since this does not render her forbidden to her husband, it is obvious that if the husband issues a warning in this manner, violating the warning does not cause her to become a *sotah*. The verse is therefore not required to exclude this case. **Rather, Abaye said:** The verse **excludes** a case **where** the husband **issued a warning to** his wife **with regard to** engaging in genital **contact** without actual penetration[49].

This *sugya* uses the phrase *pritzuta b'alma* to refer to intimate physical contact that is not intercourse. The phrase used to describe this kind of contact is "ביאה דרך אברים" — intercourse by way of [other] limbs." This includes kissing, mutual masturbation, and oral sex. However, the Gemara is here referring to actions that might take place in public. Presumably, then, they are imagining kissing and touching each other's bodies.[50]

---

[49] This translation was taken directly from the Sefaria edition of Rabbi Steinsaltz's English. Because of the complexity of these few lines, in this case, I simply cut and paste with their interpolation in order to ease the learning of this text.

[50] See the Keren Orah, Rabbi Yitzchak Minkovsky (Lithuania, 1784-1815) on the *sugya* (s.v. *amar lei Abaya pritzuta b'alma...*), who asks how these types of actions (ביאה דרך אברים) can be categorized by the Rambam (Hil. Issurei Biah 21:1) as Torah prohibitions (*lo tikr'vu*) if the Bavli calls them "mere licentiousness." He explains that the phrase as used in the Gemara here is "לענין סוטה קאמר" and not

A second place where this phrase appears in the Bavli is in regard to a woman who has a bad reputation. The presumption of this Gemara is that people only jump to conclusions based on what they can see and that, whatever the nature of public displays of affection, they will not engage in actual intercourse.

תלמוד בבלי מסכת גיטין דף פט עמוד א
אמר רבא יצא לה שם מזנה בעיר אין חוששין לה.
מ"ט? פריצותא בעלמא הוא דחזו לה.

Bavli, Gittin 89a
Rava said: If **a rumor circulated in the city** that a woman **engaged in** *z'nut*, **we are not concerned** that the rumor is true with regard to her eligibility to marry a priest. **What is the reason** for this? It is assumed that people **saw her** engage in **merely licentious behavior.**

According to Rashi[51] this "merely licentious" behavior is parallel to our case regarding *nashim mesolelot,* as this rumor is not strong enough to prohibit her from marrying a priest. The Gemara then continues and attempts to align the lenient position of Rava with Rebbi Akiva:

כתנאי: אכלה בשוק גירגרה בשוק הניקה בשוק בכולן ר"מ אומר תצא.
ר"ע אומר משישאו ויתנו בה מוזרות בלבנה.

This statement is **parallel to** one side of a dispute among the *Tannaim:* If a woman **ate in the marketplace, walked with her neck stretched forward** in an arrogant manner **in the marketplace,** or **nursed in the marketplace, with regard to all of** these cases **Rabbi Meir** says that **she must leave** her husband, since all of these behaviors are considered licentious behavior. **Rabbi Akiva says** that she must leave him only **once the women who spin [*mozerot*] by**

meant to reflect anything broader. The same might be argued in the *sugya* in Yevamot 76a. The use of the phrase "פריצותא בעלמא" is not intended to refer to a broader prohibition but is only לענין פסולי חיתון קאמר.
[51] Rashi (s.v. *shem mezanah*) says that the rumor is that she has sex with a non-Jew or a slave. See, however, the lengthy *sugya* beginning at the bottom of Yevamot 44b and only concluding at 45a regarding the status of the offspring of a Jewish woman and a non-Jew or a slave. See also Ritva here in Gittin (s.v. *amar Rava yatzah aleha...*), who explains that the rumor need not be particularly about having had sex with a non-Jew or a slave.

the moonlight converse about her having engaged in promiscuous sexual intercourse, as this indicates that the matter is well known and accepted as fact.

Rebbi Meir understands that there are certain actions that reflect on a woman in such a negative light that, even though they might only be *pritzuta b'alma,* she can be forbidden from staying married to her husband.[52] Rebbi Akiva rejects that this type of rumor necessitates divorce and asserts that only a rumor regarding intercourse with another man would rise to that level.

The three actions that Rebbi Meir outlines are certainly not forbidden; they are, at most, *"pritzuta b'alma* — mere licentiousness." These three actions are fairly common in our communities at this point: eating in the market, walking with an arrogant posture in the market, and nursing her child in the market. These three practices are clearly societally defined. While they were considered licentious behavior by the rabbis, our framework for understanding people who engage in these behaviors has shifted in our times. While there are still many Orthodox communities in which women do not nurse in public, in the vast majority of the Orthodox world it is not considered immodest for a woman to eat in a restaurant.

These public behaviors seem to create a presumption that the women in question might ultimately engage in a prohibited action. Rav Moshe seems to think the same about *nashim mesolelot.* It is clear to Rav Moshe that a woman who engages sexually with other women is also interested in sex with men. While that might be the case, there are certainly women for whom it is not.

We see the phrase "פריצותא בעלמא — mere licentiousness" in three *sugyot* in the Bavli:

1. Yevamot 76a regarding *nashim mesolelot* in explanation of why she is not forbidden to a priest (against Rav Huna).
2. Sotah 26b regarding which sexual behaviors potentially initiate *sotah* ceremony.
3. Gittin 89a regarding rumors that can prohibit a woman from marrying a priest and certain societally defined immodest behaviors.

---

[52] This seems to be the way Rav Moshe understands the position of Rav Huna in the Bavli. There is nothing inherently prohibited about this kind of behavior, but it reflects something about the person who does it that makes them suspect.

The behaviors that Rebbi Meir describes as immodest are not objectively inappropriate and certainly not *halakhically* prohibited, even if there was a time when they were unconscionable. If we accept the Bavli's categorization of *nashim mesolelot* as *pritzuta b'alma*, perhaps we can make the same argument.[53] Even though at a certain time and under certain parameters this behavior was unacceptable, that categorization can shift in a new reality.

Relationship to the Sifra

We have seen above how the Rambam subsumed the Bavli's idea of *nashim mesolelot* under the Sifra's notion of *maaseh Eretz Mitzrayim*. I previously noted that the Bavli never quotes this *drasha* regarding *maaseh Eretz Mitzrayim*. In fact, in the *sugya* in Shabbat 65a, it would have been the perfect explanation for the apparent stringency of Shmuel's father, yet it doesn't appear.

The Gemara is bothered by the fact that Shmuel's father will not permit his daughters to sleep in the same bed. Perhaps, asks the Gemara, that is because he holds like Rav Huna? But such a claim would be unreasonable because it goes against Beit Hillel and Rava! Therefore the Gemara concludes that the reason he does not want his daughters sleeping in the same bed as each other is so they don't become accustomed to sleeping with another body and therefore end up seeking the sexual company of a man.

The simplest explanation for Shmuel's father's behavior could have been that he was concerned about the interpretation of the Sifra and did not want his daughters to violate a known prohibition. Once the Rambam makes the link between *nashim mesolelot* and *maaseh Eretz Mitzrayim*, this question becomes obvious. How could the Bavli ignore an open Sifra? The answer, for the vast majority of Rishonim, is that the Bavli does not hold by the idea that there is a separate prohibition of marriage between two women called *maaseh Eretz Mitzrayim*.

This question was asked by Rabbi Yehuda Navon (d. 1761, Jerusalem) in his [54] קרית מלך רב ח״ב שאלה כו and outlined on page 39.

The same question was asked by Rav Moshe Sofer (d. 1839, known as Chatam Sofer in recognition of his major book of *responsa*) in his brief

---

[53] Many Achronim regularly refer to *nashim mesolelot* as *pritzuta b'alma*. Here is just one example:
שו"ת אבני נזר חלק אבן העזר סימן קלט ...הא לא שייך בנשים להדדי איסור משכב כלל ונשים המסוללות זו בזו פרי־
צותא בעלמא

[54] His question and answer are summarized in the back of the Metivta Shas on Shabbat in the Yalkut Biurim on *daf* 65b, page קלז. See also יד & טו אות כ סימן העזר אבן הפוסקים אוצר, where he also refers to this same text.

commentary that appears printed in the back of the standard Vilna Shas. He offers a sharp insight on the citation of the Ein Mishpat אות ל. He asks the question on the Ein Mishpat because it is a reference to the Rambam bringing the Sifra and *maaseh Eretz Mitzrayim* together. He writes:

וצע"ג דלא פריך ש"ס מידי אאבוה [דשמואל] דהא מעשה מצרים הוא

> And this needs careful consideration because the Gemara did not ask anything from [the case of] Shmuel's father regarding this being *maaseh Eretz Mitzrayim.*

The answer that the Chatam Sofer offers is that the daughters of Shmuel's father must have been minors. However, he is not satisfied by this answer, because of a father's obligation to educate his children. We learn this from the Magen Avraham (128:62), who describes a case where the daughter of a priest engaged in *z'nut* and the father bears responsibility even though she is no longer living in his home. The claim is that it was the father's responsibility to teach his daughter when she was still in his home, just like the father of Shmuel. The Chatam Sofer leaves the question בדוחק, with difficulty.

The proof that the Bavli either rejects the Sifra or simply ignores the Sifra is made even stronger by virtue of the fact that it does quote the same verse in Vayikra for other reasons. The Bavli does not interpret the general prohibition against walking in the ways of non-Jews as being particularly about sexual impropriety. In Avoda Zara 11a and Chulin 41b, the same verse, Vayikra 18:3, is used to articulate a broad prohibition of mimicking non-Jewish behaviors. In fact, Onkelos translates the word "ובחקותיהם — and in their laws" into "ובנימוסיהם — and in their manners.[55]"

The questions of the Achronim underscoring the fact that the Bavli does not refer to the Sifra, plus the fact that this very same biblical verse is used to teach us something else, reinforces the claim that the Bavli does not hold by — or perhaps even rejects — the Sifra. The fact that *rov* Rishonim comment on these texts without reference to the Sifra or the Rambam leads one to conclude that they did not think that the Sifra was significant for the purposes of *halakha.*

---

[55] See Rambam Hil. Avoda Zara chapter 11 and Yoreh Deah section 178.

C. The Marriage of an *Androginos*

1. Gemara, Rashi, and Tosafot

The *halakhic* status of the *androginos* (a person with both male and female genitalia) is an extremely complex topic in and of itself and extends beyond the scope of this essay. For my purposes, it is important to understand some of the basic questions of identity. That will lead us to analyze the positions of Rambam and Tosafot. The Rambam will then open us to a broader field of questions.

Our analysis of *androginos* begins with a complex Mishnah in Yevamot (Chapter 8 Mishnah 6)

משנה יבמות פרק ח משנה ו, דף פא ע"א

[1]...רבי יוסי ור"ש אומרים אנדרוגינוס כהן שנשא בת ישראל מאכילה בתרומה...

[2] אנדרוגינוס נושא אבל לא נישא.

[3] ר' אליעזר אומר אנדרוגינוס חייבין עליו סקילה כזכר.

Mishnah, Yevamot 8:6, page 81a

[1]...Rabbi Yossi and Rabbi Shimon say, "If a priest who is an *androginos* married an Israelite woman, he confers upon her the right to eat *teruma*...".

[2] An *androginos* may marry [a woman], but may not be married [to a man].

[3] Rabbi Eliezer says, "[If a man has relations with an] *androginos,* [he] is liable to be stoned on his account as a [man who has relations with another] man.

All of the Tannaim of the Mishnah appear to treat the *androginos* as male for all purposes: as a priest, the *androginos* can confer the right to eat food that is only permitted to priests and their families; as an Israelite, the *androginos* can marry a woman but not a man; and, finally, Rabbi Eliezer treats the *androginos* as a man for the purposes of the laws of homosexual sex.

The Gemara immediately following this Mishnah teaches of a debate between Rebbi Yochanan and Resh Lakish regarding just how effective the marriage of the priest-*androginos* can be. According to Resh Lakish, the marriage only permits the wife to eat rabbinic *teruma* and not sacrificial meats. Rebbi Yochanan takes the Mishnah at face value and asserts that, in fact, the marriage of the priest-*androginos* functions on a Torah level and the wife may even eat sacrificial meat.

The question that we must answer is this: according to those who think that an *androginos* carries some level of doubtful status as both male and female or either male or female, why is such a person permitted to marry a woman? We can understand why the *androginos* may not have sex with another man, but why is he not also forbidden from having sex with a woman?

The Gemara then takes a lengthy digression and only returns to the question of the status of the *androginos* beginning at the bottom of 82b. The Gemara continues to challenge the position of Resh Lakish, who appears to limit the efficacy of the priest-*androginos* marriage:

תלמוד בבלי מסכת יבמות דף פב עמוד ב

תנן אנדרוגינוס נושא. תני אם נשא? והא "נושא" קתני. וליטעמיך מאי "אבל לא נישא" אלא מאי "נישא" דיעבד "נושא" נמי דיעבד. אמרי לא "נושא" לכתחלה משמע, אבל "לא נישא" דיעבד נמי לא. והא מדקתני סיפא "רבי אליעזר אומר אנדרוגינוס חייבין עליו סקילה כזכר" מכלל דת"ק ספוקי מספקא ליה? בין למר בין למר מפשט פשיטא ליה. איכא ביינייהו סקילה משני מקומות: דמר סבר חייבין עליו סקילה משני מקומות. ומר סבר כזכר.

Bavli Yevamot 82b
We learned in the Mishnah: **An *androginos* may marry** a woman. **Teach**, rather: **If he married. But doesn't the** Mishnah teach **he may marry** a woman? **And according to your reasoning, what does "But he may not be married"** to a man" mean? **Rather, what is** the meaning of: He may not **be married** to a man? It means that even **after the fact** the marriage is not valid. This being the case, when the mishnah states that an *androginos* **may marry** a woman, it is **also** speaking **after the fact.** It may be **said** in response: **No;** the words **"may marry" indicate** that an *androginos* may marry a woman *ab initio*, whereas the words **"but he may not be married"** mean that his marriage to a man is **not** valid **even after the fact. But from** the fact **that** the mishnah teaches in **the latter clause: Rabbi Eliezer says** that if a man had intercourse with **an *androginos*,** he **is liable to** receive the punishment of **stoning on his account as if** he had relations with **a male**, this proves **by

inference that the first *tanna* is uncertain as to whether or not an *androginos* is considered a full-fledged male?.No, it **is obvious both to this Master and to that Master** that an *androginos* is deemed a full-fledged male. The practical difference **between them** relates to the question of whether one is liable to receive the punishment of **stoning** for inter-course with him at only one place or **at two places. As one sage,** the first *tanna*, **holds that one is liable to** be punished with **stoning on** an *androginos*'s **account** for intercourse **at two places,** whether he penetrated him anally, in the manner of homosexual intercourse, or through his female organ. Since the *androginos* is deemed a male, one is liable to be punished with stoning for intercourse at either place. **And one sage,** Rabbi Eliezer, **holds** that one is liable to be punished with stoning for relations with an *androginos* only if he penetrated him anally, **as if** he were **a male.**

As Rashi (s.v. *tenan androginos noseh l'khat'chila*) explains, the opening question argues against Resh Lakish. The language of the Mishnah implies that the *androginos* may marry a woman *ab initio* and that the wedding is considered a complete marriage. Why, then, does Resh Lakish only permit her to eat *teruma* on a rabbinic level? Tosafot (s.v. *tenan androginos noseh*) explain that the word לכתחילה (*ab initio*) as it appears in this *sugya* means נישואין ודאין (certain marriage).

This Tosafot's second point in this same passage brings us back to the question of *nashim mesolelot*. There he writes:

תוספות מסכת יבמות דף פב עמוד ב, "תנן אנדרוגינוס נושא"
אבל אין לפרש דמדקדק מדשרי לכתחלה לישא ולא אסרינן ליה לכ־
תחלה מספק נשים המסוללות זו בזו.
דמאחר דמאכיל לר"ל בתרומה בזמן הזה דרבנן, לא מסתבר לאוסרו
בתחלה מטעם זה.

Tosafot Yevamot 82b, s.v. *Tenan androginos noseh*
But we should not interpret [this as saying] that we can infer that since they are permitted *ab initio* to marry and we do not prohibit them *ab initio* because of the *safek* of

nashim hamesolelot.[56] Since [even] according to Resh Lakish [when a priest-*androginos*] marries, [their partner] can
eat rabbinic *teruma*. It does not make sense to prohibit
[the marriage] from the outset because of this reason [of
nashim mesolelot].

These two sentences of *Tosafot* contain an unstated assumption about the
nature of *nashim mesolelot*. In order to discern what they are taking for
granted, we need to read very carefully. First they explain what we should
not think. We should not infer that if we had a doubt regarding the status of
the *androginos* — male or female — then we ought to forbid their marriage
to a woman because of *safek nashim mesolelot*. Such an inference is impossible because even Resh Lakish permits the *androginos* to marry a woman,
as the Mishnah says explicitly, but simply limits what she can eat. Therefore
safek nashim mesolelot must be less of a problem than a ספק זרה (a woman
who is married to a priest, but whose relationship is suspect) eating תרומה
מדרבנן (rabbinic *teruma*). The strong implication of Tosafot here is that there
is no real prohibition associated with *nashim mesolelot*[57].

Rabbi Nachman Kahane in his Mei Menuchot on this passage in Tosafot
states it very simply:

דחיית החשש ל'נשים מסוללות זו בזו' אינו קשה לריש לקיש, כי הצורך
לתקן נישואין לאנדרוגינוס גובר על החשש ל'נשים מסוללות זו בזו'
שאינה להלכה (לעיל עו,א 'נשים מסוללות זו בזו... פריצותא בעלמא')
ומה עוד שנישואין אלא מתירים לאכול רק תרומה דרבנן.

The rejection of the concern of *nashim mesolelot* is not
problematic [even] for Resh Lakish because the need to
establish a marriage for an *androginos* overcomes the concern for '*nashim mesolelot one with another*,' which we do
not maintain for practical purposes of Jewish Law (See
earlier 76a *nashim mesolelot... pritzuta b'alma*). And even

---

[56] This sentence is extremely difficult and appears to be missing a phrase. See the Metivta Shas Biurei
Tosafot for an attempt to fill in the gaps.

[57] See the שו"ת צפנת פענח סימן קסד (R. Yosef Rosen, the Rogotchover, d. 1936) who, in addressing the
question of whether women are bound by the prohibition of the wanton destruction of male seed, refers
to this passage in Tosafot and says simply:
"ע' ביבמות דף ע"ו ע"א גבי נשים מסוללות, ודף פ"ב ע"ב בתוספות דלא אסור בספק."
This *teshuva* of the צפנת פענח is also quoted in the אוצר הפוסקים אב"ע סימן כ אות טו regarding the question
of the potential level of prohibition of *mesolelot* within the Rambam.

more so that this marriage only permits the consumption of rabbinic *teruma.*

This formulation is very powerful, as Rabbi Kahane understands that the human need to get married has *halakhic* implications. We will return to this passage in Tosafot when we unpack the various *psakim* of the Rambam on this matter. The Gemara then continues to try to define the status of the *androginos*:

אמר רב ליתא למתניתין מקמי ברייתא. דתניא: רבי יוסי אומר אנדרו־
גינוס בריה בפני עצמה הוא ולא הכריעו בו חכמים אם זכר אם נקבה.
אדרבה ליתא לברייתא מקמי מתניתין. מדשבקיה רבי יוסי לבר זוגיה
ש״מ הדר ביה. ושמואל אמר ליתא לברייתא מקמי מתניתין. אדרבה
ליתא למתניתין מקמי ברייתא דהא שמעינן ליה לשמואל דחייש לי־
חידאה. הני מילי כי לא מתעקרא מתניתין אבל כי מתעקרא מתניתין
לא חייש. אמרי בי רב משמיה דרב הלכה כרבי יוסי באנדרוגינוס...

Rav said: The Mishnah here, which states that according to Rabbi Yosei a priest who is an *androginos* enables his wife to eat *teruma,* **is not** to be relied upon **in the presence of a *baraita*** that teaches otherwise. **As it is taught** in a *baraita* that **Rabbi Yosei says:** An *androginos* **is a creature unto himself, and the sages did not determine whether he is a male or a female.** He is consequently prohibited from marrying a woman, and if he does so he does not enable her to eat *teruma.* The Gemara asks: **On the contrary,** say that **the *baraita* is not** to be relied upon **in the presence of the Mishnah** here, as *baraitot* are generally considered less authoritative than *mishnayot.* The Gemara answers: **From** the fact **that Rabbi Yosei left his colleague,** Rabbi Shimon, as the Mishnah's ruling is attributed to both Rabbi Yosei and Rabbi Shimon whereas the teaching of the *baraita* is reported only in the name of Rabbi Yosei, **learn from this** that Rabbi Yosei **retracted** his original opinion that he had maintained together with Rabbi Shimon and reached a different conclusion. **And Shmuel said** the reverse: **The *baraita* is not** to be relied upon **in the presence of the Mishnah** here. The Gemara asks: **On the contrary,** say that **the Mishnah** here **is not** to be relied upon **in the presence**

of the *baraita,* as we have **heard that Shmuel takes into consideration** even **an individual** dissenting opinion appearing in a *baraita*. The Gemara answers: **This applies only when the Mishnah** itself is **not** thereby **uprooted,** as the *baraita* merely adds to it. **But when the Mishnah is uprooted** by a contrary statement taught in a *baraita,* **he does not take** it **into consideration.** The Sages of **the school of Rav said in the name of Rav** that the *halakha* **is in accordance with** the opinion of **Rabbi Yosei,** both **with regard to** the *halakha* of **an** *androginos...*

There is a debate as to which opinion of Rebbi Yossi Rav intends to support. Rashi (s.v. *Halakha k'Rebbi Yossi*) says that this passage refers to the Rebbi Yossi of the Mishnah and not of the *baraita*. In fact, Tosafot (s.v. *Halakha k'Rebbi Yossi*) concurs with Rashi's *psak* in accordance with Rebbi Yossi of the Mishnah.

2. Rambam and Rashba

This Mishnah on its face treats the *androginos* as a man. However, Rebbi Yossi in the *baraita* claims that an *androginos* is the subject of some doubt. Rambam claims that Rav and his *beit midrash* meant to *pasken* in accordance with the Rebbi Yossi of the *baraita* that an *androginos* is its own category, "בריה בפני עצמה." Rambam (Hil. Ishut 2:24) clearly states his approach here.[58]

רמב"ם אישות פרק ב הלכה כד

מי שיש לו איברי זכרות ואיברי נקבות הוא הנקרא אנדרוגינוס והוא ספק אם הוא זכר אם נקבה. ואין לו סימן שיודע בו אם הוא זכר ודאי או נקבה ודאית לעולם.

Rambam, Hil. Ishut 2:24

A person who has both male sexual organs and female sexual organs is called an *androginos,* and there is a doubt if he is [to be considered] male or female. And he will never

---

[58] The Rosh (Yevamot 8:8) *paskens* that an *androginos* is considered fully male. However, it seems that the majority of Rishonim *pasken* like the Rambam. See Shulchan Aruch Even HaEzer 44:5 with the Rema there who brings the Rosh. See also Shulchan Aruch 22:12, where the Rema remained quiet. See also the Tzitz Eliezer 3:13 where he brings together many of the issues.

have a sign that is knowable [that would clarify] whether he
is [to be considered] male for certain or female for certain.

Because Rambam decides in accordance with Rebbi Yossi in the *baraita,* he
cannot *pasken* like Rebbi Yochanan that the wife of a priest-*androginos* may
eat sacrificial meat. He does not even want to go as far as Resh Lakish, and
he *paskens* that the wife of priest-*androginos* may not eat *teruma*:

רמב"ם הלכות תרומות פרק ז הלכה יד
...אנדרוגינוס: עבדיהן אוכלין, אבל לא נשותיהן.

Rambam, Laws of *Terumot,* Chapter 7 *Halakha* 14
[Priest-]*Androginos:* their slaves eat, but their wives do not.

Even though the priest-*androginos* can exert complete ownership of a slave,
according to the Rambam he cannot fully marry a woman. Therefore his
slaves do eat the sacrificial meat, but his wife may not (even rabbinic *teruma*). In addition, Rambam says explicitly that an *androginos* may marry a
woman — as the Mishnah also states unequivocally.

רמב"ם הלכות איסורי ביאה פרק א הלכה טו
[אחד הבא על הזכר או] הבא על אנדרוגינוס דרך זכרותו חייב [ואם
בא עליו דרך נקבותו פטור]...
והאנדרוגינוס מותר לישא אשה.

Rambam, Laws of Prohibited Intercourse, Chapter 1 *Halakha* 15
[One who has sex with a male or] who has sex with an
androginos through his male sexual organs is liable [and
if he had sex with him through his female sexual organs,
he is not liable]... and the *androginos* is allowed to marry
a woman.

It is this final *psak* that reflects something about Rambam's approach to
nashim mesolelot. Even though the *androginos*'s sex is the subject of a doubt,
they may nonetheless marry a woman. Just as Tosafot above appear to say
almost no prohibition applies to *nashim mesolelot,* this passage in the Rambam concurs: if there is a prohibition, it is very limited. The most basic claim
that we can make for Rambam is that he must think that *nashim mesolelot*

is prohibited at a lower level than *mishkav zachar*. While that may appear obvious to many people, it is significant to note that, from within this section of the Mishneh Torah, he clearly thinks that *nashim mesolelot* is not a Torah prohibition.

When taken all together, these collective *psakim* of the Rambam leave one wondering what he thinks about *nashim mesolelot*. The Rashba was the first to be bothered by this issue:

חידושי הרשב"א מסכת יבמות דף פג עמוד א

והרמב"ם ז"ל פסק בחבורו הגדול (פ"ז תרומות הי"ד) ובפרושי המשנה אשר לו כר' יוסי דברייתא דאמר בריה בפני עצמה הוא ולפיכך אינו מאכיל בתרומה לפי שהוא ספק וספק איסורא לחומרא. ופסק (פ"א הל' איסו"ב הט"ו) כר' אלעזר דאמר חייבין עליו סקילה כזכר. ולא ידעתי היאך יתקיימו שני הפסקים הללו?... ועוד קשה לי שהוא ז"ל כתב (פ"א הל' איסו"ב הט"ו) דנושא לכתחילה. ואי ספיקא הוא איך נושא לכתחלה, דלמא נקבה היא ואין אשה נושאת אשה?...וצל"ע.

Chidushei HaRashba, Yevamot 83a

And the Rambam, of blessed memory, ruled in his major opus (Hil. Terumot 7:14) and in his explanations of the Mishnah that Rebbi Yossi said that [the *androginos*] is a creature unto himself and therefore does not cause [it to be permissible for his wife] to eat *teruma* because of a *safek,* and a *safek* about a prohibition causes [a ruling that is in accord with] stringency. And he ruled (Hil. Issurei Biah 1:15) like Rebbe Elazar, who said that [a man who has sex with him is] liable to receive the punishment of] stoning on his account as with a male. And I do not know how these two rulings can coexist.... And it is also difficult for me that [Rambam] of blessed memory says that [the *androginos*] can marry [a woman] *ab initio*, for what if [the *androginos*] is [to be considered] female, and a woman does not marry a woman.... And this requires analysis.

The Rashba here points out that if indeed an *androginos* might be a woman then, at least for the Rambam, they should be prohibited from marrying a woman. There are two main answers offered to this question by commentaries on the page of the Rambam.

The Magid Mishneh (Rabbi Vidal of Tolosa, Spain, d. c. 1360, Barcelona) in Hil. Issurei Biah, addresses the question first. He says:

מגיד משנה הלכות איסורי ביאה פרק א הלכה טו

...ומ"ש והאנדרוגינוס מותר לישא אשה הוא כסתם מתני' דהתם (יבמות דף פ"א) דתני אנדרוגינוס נושא אבל לא נישא. ודעת רבינו אף על פי שהוא ספק וקידושיו ספק כמו שנזכר פ"ד מהלכות אישות אעפ"כ נושא לכתחילה. שאע"פ שאין אשה נושאת אשה אנדרוגינוס נושא הוא אשה, דהא חזינן דרחמנא רבייה[59] לענין משכב זכור. ואף על פי שאשה אינה נושאת אשה, ונשים המסוללות זו בזו אסור הוא, כמו שנזכר פרק כ"א, לענין זה אנדרוגינוס כזכר הוא וזהו דעת רבינו.

Magid Mishneh, Hil. Issurei Biah 1:15
*And that which [Rambam] wrote, "And the *androginos* is permitted to marry a woman" is in accordance with the anonymous Mishnah (Yevamot 81a) which taught, "An *androginos* may marry [a woman], but may not be married [to a man]." And our teacher [Rambam] thinks that even though he is of doubtful [gender] status] and his marriage is doubtful, as stated in the fourth chapter of Hil. Ishut, nonetheless, he may marry a woman *ab initio*. For even though a woman may not marry another woman, and *nashim hamesolelot* is prohibited, as [Rambam] mentioned in chapter twenty one, for this matter an *androginos* is considered to be like a male. This is the opinion of our teacher [Rambam].

The Magid Mishneh's point is that since for the purposes of anal sex we consider the *androginos* to be a male, we also consider him to be male as it relates to the potential prohibition of *mesolelot* in this relationship. The *kiddushin* may be built on a doubt, but regarding his intimate physical behavior, the *androginos* is considered male.

This reading does not reflect anything specific about the nature of *mesolelot* for the Rambam. The Lechem Mishneh (Rabbi Avraham Hiyya de Boton, Salonica, Constantinople, d. 1603-1609) gives a different answer:

---

[59] See Yevamot 83b where the Gemara says, "**Bar Hamedurei explained it to me,** based on an allusion to this *halakha* found in the Bible. The verse states: **"And you shall not lie with a male as with a woman** [*mishkevei isha*]" (Leviticus 18:22). What male has two manners of lying? You must say that this is referring to **an** *androginos*."

לחם משנה הלכות איסורי ביאה פרק א הלכה טו
אחד הבא על הזכר וכו'...ע"כ משמע דלמ"ד ספק, דהוי ר"ל, אינו
נושא לכתחלה. וי"ל דהא מפרש כפירוש התוספות דמai דפריך הוא
מדקאמר נושא משמע נישואין גמורין דאי לא היה לו לומר אנדרוגינוס
שקידש קידושיו קידושין.

Lechem Mishnah, Hil. Issurei Biah, 1:15
According to Resh Lakish, who says that [the status of
the *androginos* is a matter of]doubt] the *androginos* may
not marry [anyone] *ab initio*. And we can say that Rambam understands like the explanation of Tosafot. That the
word "he may marry" means that they can have a complete
marriage. For if that were not the intention, the Mishnah
should have said, "An *androginos* who betrothed, their betrothal is effective."

The reading of the Lechem Mishneh, linking Rambam and Tosafot, must
ultimately mean that *mesolelot* cannot be a Torah prohibition. It may also
lower the level of potential prohibition beneath even a rabbinic concern, as it
must be viewed as less of an issue than a potential non-priest eating *teruma*.

3. Cheker Halakha, Noda B'Yehuda, Chatam Sofer
We can now move to the late 18th- and early 19th-century material that
deals with the question of the marriage of an *androginos* on a practical level.
Though it is difficult to say with certainty, one gets the sense that Rambam
was dealing with abstract categories and never had to address an actual
case of an *androginos* who wanted to get married. The same is not true in
the following cases.

In 1779, two of the greatest *poskim* of the generation were faced with
the same practical case of an *androginos* who asked to get married. Rabbi
Elazar ben Elazar Kallir,[60] author of Ohr Chadash and Cheker Halakha,
began to serve as the chief rabbi of Rechnitz in 1768. He received a letter
from the leaders of the city of Vishnitz on February 11, 1779 asking for his
direction in this matter. He then wrote a letter to his more senior colleague

---
[60] He claimed to have been related to the *paytan* Eliezer HaKallir. His father, Elazar, died while his
mother was pregnant, so he carries the same name. He was also the grandson of Rabbi Meir Eisenstadt,
author of the responsum *Panim Me'irot* as well as a commentary on the Chumash and the five Megillot
known as Kotnot Or. The Kotnot Or was published together with Rav Elazar's commentary on the
Torah, Ohr Chadash.

Rabbi Jeffrey Fox

and chief rabbi of the great city of Prague, Rabbi Yechezkel Landau, the author of the Noda B'Yehuda. Rav Elazar ben Elazar waited for the answer from the Noda B'Yehuda and then added his own response. It is to those two *teshuvot* that we now turn.

The Noda B'Yehuda's *teshuva* is the first entry in Even HaEzer, Mahadura Tinyana. He begins by quoting the Mishnah in Yevamot 81a together with the Gemara there, page 82b, with the debate between Rebbi Yochanan and Resh Lakish about the marriage of the priest-*androginos*. He then goes on to refer to Rambam's complicated *psak* that permits an *androginos* to marry a woman but does not permit the wife of the priest-*androginos* to eat *teruma*, and *paskens* like Rebbi Yossi in the *baraita* that an *androginos*'s status is one of doubt. He then notes that the Rashba also picked up on this same inconsistency. Finally, he brings the Magid Mishneh's resolution and pushes back against that approach.

Then the Noda B'Yehuda writes:

שו"ת נודע ביהודה מהדורא תניינא - אבן העזר סימן א

ועוד נלענ"ד דרמב"ם סבר כפירוש שפירשו התוס' בדף פ"ב ע"ב ד"ה תנן וכו' דבשביל אשה נושאת אשה אין סברא כלל לאסור אנדרוגינוס מלישא. ואף שהתוס' כתבו כן לר"ש דסבר מאכיל בתרומה דרבנן ולהרמב"ם אינו מאכיל כלל. סובר הרמב"ם מצד הסברא אין שייך לאסור אנדרוגינוס מטעם נשים המסוללות. כיון שמשמש דרך זכרותו אינו בכלל מעשה ארץ מצרים....

Noda B'Yehuda Tinyana, Even HaEzer 1

And it also appears to me, in my humble opinion, that Rambam thinks like the explanation of Tosafot (Yevamot 82b, s.v. *tenan,* etc.) that the concern of a "woman marrying a woman" is not at all a logical reason to prohibit an *androginos* from marrying. And even though Tosafot wrote this in relation to Resh Lakish, who holds that the priest-*androginos* permits his wife to eat Rabbinic *teruma,* and according to Rambam [the priest-*androginos* does not permit his wife] to eat any [*teruma*]. The Rambam holds, based on logic, that it is not relevant to prohibit the [marriage of an] *androginos* because of *nashim mesolelot.* Because he has relations by means of his male organ, it is not within the category of *maaseh Eretz Mitzrayim....*

Simply put, the Noda B'Yehuda reads like the Lechem Mishneh and con-
nects Rambam to Tosafot.[61] This is significant because, for Tosafot, the
concerns about *mesolelot* are fairly circumscribed. Ultimately, as we saw
in Tosafot, *mesolelot* has to be understood as less than the concern about
a woman who is a ספק זרה (a potential non-priest, because her *kiddushin*
is doubtful) eating Rabbinic *teruma*. If nothing else, one can claim with
confidence that *mesolelot* cannot be a Torah prohibition — even within the
system of the Rambam.[62]

The *teshuva* of the Cheker Halakha[63] begins with the same cluster of
source material — the Mishnah in Yevamot (81a) together with the Gemara
there (82b) as well as the Rambam and the question of the Rashba. He then
refers to the answers of both the Magid Mishneh and the Lechem Mishneh.

The Cheker Halakha is also drawn to the answer of the Lechem Mishneh,
which links Rambam and Tosafot, thereby limiting the potential prohibition
of *mesolelot*. His elaboration is helpful in clarifying the positions of both
Rambam and Tosafot:

לפי התירוץ של הרב לחם משנה דהרמב"ם קאי בשיטת תוספות, דאין
לאסור לכתחילה משום איסור מסוללות כיון דמאכיל בתרומה דרבנן...
ואין לפרש בכוונת התוספות דגבי אנדרוגינוס לא שייך כלל איסור
מסוללות מחמת שהוא משמש דרך זכרות, זה ליתא, דא"כ לא הוצרך
התוספות לדמותו לאכילת תרומה כלל...

According to the answer of the Lechem Mishneh that Rambam agrees with Tosafot that we should not prohibit [the
marriage of an *androginos*] because of the prohibition of
mesolelot since [the priest-*androginos* permits his wife to
eat] rabbinic *teruma*... And we cannot say that according

---

[61] It is not clear to me why the Noda B'Yehuda does not refer to the answer given by the Lechem Mishneh.
[62] The Noda B'Yehuda *paskens* the actual question regarding the *androginos* that he is permitted to marry
a woman but may not recite the *brachot* of *erusin* because of the doubtful nature of his status, which
has led to the *androginos* having permission to marry but not being commanded or obligated to marry.
He wrote, "ולכן נלע"ד שמותר לו לישא, אמנם הברכות לא יברכו כי אינו מצווה לישא רק מותר לישא." The *teshuva*
concludes with an analogy to the wedding of two *chershim* at which the common *minhag* used to be to
have a double wedding, for a hearing couple and the two *chershim* together, and make the *brachot* for
the hearing couple in the presence of the *chershim*. In the final two lines, he repeats his recommenda-
tion, "ולכן אנדרוגינוס הזה יכול לישא אשה ויקדש אותה בחופה וקידושין אבל בלא ברכת אירוסין. ומה טוב לכוין שתהיה
חופתה כאחד עם חתן אחר וכלה שלו וישמע ברכות של החתן ההוא." See Igrot Moshe, Even HaEzer 1:87, where he
deals with the question of the marriage of *chershim* and tries to clarify the *psak* of the Noda B'Yehuda.
[63] Rabbi Elazar ben Elazar. Originally published in 1838 (Vienna), about 37 years after his passing, together with an approbation of Rabbi Moshe Sofer. It was published again in 1898 (Munkatch) and then
reprinted in the back of the *Machon Yerushalyim* edition of the *teshuvot* of the Noda B'Yehuda (1993/4).

to Tosafot the prohibition of *mesolelot* does not apply to an *androginos* because he has relations by means of his male organ; this is wrong — for if this were the case, Tosafot would not have needed to make the analogy to Rabbinic *teruma*.

He then brings up the Magid Mishneh's combination of Rashi and the Rivan that defines *mesolelot* as exchanging semen and says:

> או יאמר דאף אם נפרש שיטת רש"י והריב"ם [צ"ל: ריב"ן] אין כאן
> איסור כלל, מ"מ י"ל דהיינו דוקא שני נשים מסוללות שלא שייך הטלת
> זרע כ"א מה שקבלו מבעליהן, משא"כ באנרוגינוס שמטיל זרע עצמו...

Or you could say that even if we explain according to Rashi and Rivam [Rivan], there is no prohibition here at all. Nevertheless, one could say that this is only with two women who are *mesolelot* and there is no possibility of exchanging semen, which is not the case with an *androginos,* who gives his own semen.

Here he says quite clearly that according to both Rashi and the Rivan there is no prohibition of two women engaging in intimate sexual behavior as long as there is no semen involved.

He refers to the approach of the Prisha several times throughout the *teshuva*. His understanding of the Prisha as commentary on both the Tur and the Rambam is very important. The Rambam's subsuming of *mesolelot* into *maaseh Eretz Mitzrayim* opened up the possibility for the greatest potential prohibition. However, the Cheker Halakha's insistence that the Prisha can be read on the Rambam leads to the following approach:

> ואע"פ שכ' המ"מ בפ' כ"א מהא"ב [ה"ח], בדעת רש"י שהוא כפירוש
> הריב"ם [צ"ל: ריב"ן] דלעיל [ע"ו ע"א], דמסוללת היינו שמטילות זרע
> בעליהן זה לזה. י"ל דדוקא התם לענין פיסול כהונה הואי דמפרש הכי,
> אבל איסור יש גם בפנויות, שהרי חשיב להדי' בספרי הלאו דכמעשה
> ארץ מצרים שהיתה אשה נושאת אשה, והיינו משום מיעוט קיום העולם
> כמ"ש הפרישה [אב"ע סימן כ אות יא].

And even though the Magid Mishneh wrote that the opinion of Rashi is like the Rivam [Rivan] — that *mesolelot*
refers to transferring semen from their husbands to each
other — we can say that this is only regarding [the women's]
status relative to marrying a priest, but there is a prohibition with single women as well, for behold the prohibition
of *maaseh Eretz Mitzrayim* is listed explicitly in the Sifra,
that one woman would marry another woman. And this
is prohibited because it limits the population of the world,
as the Prisha wrote.

This is among the most lenient ways of reading the Rambam that appears in
the *teshuva* literature. Here, the Cheker Halakha takes the Prisha's reading
to its conclusion. The only reason for the prohibition of two women marrying each other is that they are not able to have children. We are blessed to
live at a time when this is simply no longer the reality of two women living
together. They can, if they are so inclined, seek to have children through
artificial insemination.[64]

Both the Cheker Halakha and the Noda B'Yehuda accept the Lechem
Mishneh's reading of the Rambam, which links his approach to Tosafot,
thereby limiting the potential prohibition of *mesolelot*. When we include the
Prisha as a reading of the Rambam, the concerns are made even lower in
a committed monogamous relationship that seeks to have children. Now I
turn to the Chatam Sofer to see how he weighed this potential prohibition.

Rabbi Moshe Sofer addresses the question of the marriage of an *androginos* and *nashim mesolelot* in a short essay on *bikkurim* simply entitled פרק
אנדרוגינוס.[65] He begins by referring to a second answer offered by Tosafot
(Yevamot 82b s.v. *d'tenan*) regarding an *androginos* marrying a woman,

---

[64] See the very important *teshuva* of Rav David Bigman regarding the permissibility of a single woman
to have a child through artificial insemination. In the opening paragraphs, Rav Bigman writes, "We are
faced with a reality that *Hazal* would not recognize. It never occurred to them that a single woman
could become pregnant outside the context of a sexual encounter. As a result, this question did not arise
until our time." The same is true of our topic as well. It never could have occurred to Chazal or the
Rambam or the Prisha that two *frum* women would want to live together and start their own family. See
the website for the Lindenbaum Center for Halakhic Studies: https://library.yctorah.org/lindenbaum/
rachels-cry-single-women-pru-urvu/
[65] This article first appeared in a book called ילקוט דניאל published in Pressburg 5763 (1912/3). It appears
to have been sent as a letter in Av of 5562 (August 1803), just twenty-five years after the debate between
the Cheker Halakha and the Noda B'Yehuda. It was subsequently published again in New York in 5721
(1961/2) in a book called שיר השירים, which gathered a series of handwritten manuscripts of the Chatam
Sofer and republished them. When the *chiddushim* of the Chatam Sofer on Shas were more systemat-
ically reprinted in the 1980s, this same piece appeared in the back of Brachot as well on Yevamot 82.

where Tosafot claims that perhaps we need to be told that there is a mitzvah to get married that overrides the potential prohibition of *mesolelot*.

The Chatam Sofer concludes the paragraph with the following:

וי"ל דא"כ מאי קמ"ל פשיטה דמחייב בכל המצוות מספיקא,דאין לומר
נושא אצטריכא ליה דסד"א לתסר משום נשים מסוללות, ז"א, הא כבר
כתבו תוס' [יבמות שם] השתא תרומה בזה"ז מאכיל (יין לי') משום נשים
מסוללות ניחוש, בתמיה, שהוא קל וצניעות בעלמא וא"ש.

> We could say that there is nothing to learn here, because
> it is obvious that we obligate [an *androginos*] in all the
> mitzvot due to *safek*. But we have to say that we obligate
> [an *androginos*] to marry lest [otherwise] we think that
> we prohibit [the *androginos*] to marry because of *nashim*
> *mesolelot*, which is not the case. For behold Tosafot has
> already written that [the priest-*androginos*] permits [his
> wife] to eat rabbinic *teruma*, [so how] would there be any
> reason to be concerned about *mesolelot*? they asked. For
> it [*mesolelot*] is a light matter and only an issue of *tzniut*?

Here again we see that Tosafot's reading of the *sugya* leads to limitation of the potential prohibition of *mesolelot*. The Chatam Sofer does not go so far as to see that it is permitted, but he downplays the prohibition by describing it as "only a concern of modesty."

The Cheker Halakha, Noda B'Yehuda, and Chatam Sofer wrote within 24 years of each other, from 1779 to 1803. The most important implication of this material is that they all agree that, even according to the Rambam, *mesolelot* can only be considered a potential rabbinic violation. They also read Tosafot as lowering the concern below even that level. They are not particularly concerned with *maaseh Eretz Mitzrayim* and treat the position of Rashi and Tosafot separate from the Rambam.

In short, this group of Achronim confirms the idea that the reading of Rashi and Tosafot can stand on its own in opposition to the Rambam. In addition, they lower the level of concern even within the Rambam. Ultimately, when we juxtapose the Cheker Halakha, Noda B'Yehuda, Chatam Sofer, Aruch LaNer, and Rav Moshe, it becomes clear that even the most stringent reading of the potential prohibition of *mesolelot* still only relates to it as a rabbinic restriction lower than the concern of someone eating rabbinic *teruma* who might not be permitted to do so.

Nashim Mesolelot

Like the Aruch LaNer and Ishei Yisrael, this group does not clearly articulate the nature of the prohibition of *mesolelot* as it might apply to two single women who are seeking to live together and build a family within the framework of a committed monogamous relationship. The Prisha's approach to the Rambam and Tur implies that such a family would be permitted.

III. Decision-Making: Where can we go from here?

A. Framing My Potential Conclusions: Rashbi Emerging from the Cave

The Gemara in Shabbat 33a tells the mythic tale of Rebbi Shimon bar Yochai, who spent a period of time in a cave with his son. Before Rashbi and his son descend into the cave, a group of rabbis chatting about the Romans is introduced:

יתבי רבי יהודה ורבי יוסי ורבי שמעון, ויתיב יהודה בן גרים גבייהו.
פתח רבי יהודה ואמר: כמה נאים מעשיהן של אומה זו: תקנו שווקים,
תקנו גשרים, תקנו מרחצאות. רבי יוסי שתק. נענה רבי שמעון בן יוחאי
ואמר: כל מה שתקנו - לא תקנו אלא לצורך עצמן, תקנו שווקין -
להושיב בהן זונות, מרחצאות - לעדן בהן עצמן, גשרים - ליטול מהן
מכס. הלך יהודה בן גרים וסיפר דבריהם, ונשמעו למלכות. אמרו:
יהודה שעילה - יתעלה, יוסי ששתק - יגלה לציפורי, שמעון שגינה
- יהרג.

Rebbi Yehudah, Rebbi Yose, and Rebbi Shimon [bar Yochai] were sitting, and Yehudah ben Gerim was sitting near them. Rebbi Yehudah opened and said, "How fine are the works of this nation [the Romans]! They established (*tiknu*) markets, they established bridges, they established bathhouses." Rebbi Yose was silent. Rebbi Shimon bar Yochai responded, "All that they established, they established for their own benefit. They built marketplaces — to set harlots in them, bathhouses — to delight in themselves, — bridges, to collect taxes." Yehuda ben Gerim went and related their talk, and it became known to the government. They said, "Yehuda, who exalted us, shall be exalted; Yose, who was silent, shall be exiled to Sepphoris; Shimon, who disparaged, shall be executed."

These great rabbis gathered together and spoke of Roman authorities. Rebbi Yehuda is appreciative of the government's role in society: building markets, bridges, and bathhouses. However, Rebbi Shimon disparages the Romans as only building the economy for their own benefit. Their markets are really for prostitutes, the bridges for taxes, and the bathhouses to beautify themselves.

As a result of this comment, Rebbi Shimon is forced into hiding, together with his son. First they hide in the *beit midrash* and then in a cave for thirteen years. When they are eventually goaded out of the cave by none other than Elijah the prophet, they are not prepared to be a part of the physical world. Each time Rebbi Shimon sees people engaging with the physical world, his eyes burn them. He and his son return to the cave for another year to gain a healthier perspective on the life of this world.

Upon exiting the cave this time, his son, Rebbi Elazar, is no longer able to accept the physical world. However, Rebbi Shimon teaches his son of the beauty of rushing to prepare for the physical pleasures of Shabbat.

Toward the end of the story, the Gemara debates what it means that Yaakov returned to Shechem *shalem*. The Amoraim say:

ויבא יעקב שלם ואמר רב: שלם בגופו, שלם בממונו, שלם בתורתו.
(בראשית לג) ויחן את פני העיר אמר רב: מטבע תיקן להם, ושמואל אמר:
שווקים תיקן להם, ורבי יוחנן אמר: מרחצאות תיקן להם.

And Jacob came whole (shalem) (Gen. 33:18). And Rav said, "Whole in his body, whole in his money, whole in his Torah." *And he was gracious to the city* (Gen 33:18). Rav said, "He established *(tiken)* coinage for them." And Shmuel said, "He established markets for them." And Rebbi Yochanan said, "He established bathhouses for them."

Here the Gemara returns to three familiar features of building an economy: coinage, markets, and bathhouses. These parallel the three ideas that were originally debated and degraded by Rebbi Shimon. Only now, after Rashbi's fourteen years in the cave and learning to appreciate the physical world, does the *sugya* remind us of the importance of these very items.

The *Sifra* that introduces us to *maaseh Eretz Mitzrayim* begins with a strawman question.

כְּמַעֲשֵׂה אֶרֶץ מִצְרַיִם... וּכְמַעֲשֵׂה אֶרֶץ כְּנַעַן... לֹא תַעֲשׂוּ. יָכוֹל לֹא יִבְנוּ
בְנְיָנוּת וְלֹא יִטְּעוּ נְטִיעוֹת כְּמוֹתָם?

"The practices of the Land of Egypt... or of the Land of
Canaan... You shall not copy." Could it mean that we may
not build buildings or plant plantings like them?

The Sifra asks the same question that Rebbi Yehuda asked and that ultimately led to Rebbi Shimon hiding in the cave for 14 years. It took Rebbi
Shimon a long time to learn that, in fact, building buildings, planting trees,
and designing an economy are essential for the world to survive. He needed
to go back into the cave and reconsider the outlook he had been cultivating
during those first 13 years in order to gain a deeper and truer appreciation
of the physical world.

The Torah with which he emerged from the cave originally was so powerful that he had no patience for the physical world and therefore was invol-
untarily destroying what he judged unfavorably. The *sugya* tells us that he
had to go back into the cave and learn Torah again in order to stop burning
up the lived physical life of the Jewish People.

We are living in a time when too many great *rabbanim* and *poskim* view
Torah through a lens that destroys the lives of gay women (and men). The
Gemara is trying to teach us that sometimes, even after many years of deep
learning, there is a need to go back into the cave and rethink our approach.
If your Torah is wreaking destruction through the judgment it serves on
others in whose place you have never stood, you at least need to begin to
imagine a different lens through which to understand Torah. You need to go
back into the cave in order to come out with a more refined approach that
appreciates that which you viewed cynically. You need to find the positive
in phenomena whose negative aspects were your focus until now. You need
to open your eyes, without fire, and turn a loving, lifesaving gaze upon Jews
who seek to fulfill God's will. We dare not pervert the Torah, but it is our
holy obligation to do our best to understand the Divine will, as expressed
through the language of *halakha*, in a way that does not destroy people's
lives.

There may be instances in which, no matter how much time is spent
in the cave, we still cannot find a way to integrate new thinking into the
normative boundaries of *halakha*. At those moments, we must be able to
say that we submit to the will of the Creator of the World, the One who

revealed the Torah to Moshe on Sinai. In those moments, perhaps, we are left with only tears.

At those times we are left with Daniel the tailor:

ויקרא רבה (וילנא) פרשה לב: ח

דָּבָר אַחֵר, וַיֵּצֵא בֶּן אִשָּׁה יִשְׂרְאֵלִית, הֲדָא הוּא דִכְתִיב (קהלת ד, א): וְשַׁבְתִּי אֲנִי וָאֶרְאֶה אֶת כָּל הָעֲשׁוּקִים, דָּנִיֵּאל חַיָּטָא פָּתַר קְרָיָה בַּמַּמְזֵרִים, (קהלת ד, א): וְהִנֵּה דִּמְעַת הָעֲשׁוּקִים, אֲבוֹתָם שֶׁל אֵלּוּ עוֹבְרֵי עֲבֵרוֹת, וְאִילֵּין עֲלוּבַיָּא מָה אִכְפַּת לְהוֹן, כָּךְ אָבִיו שֶׁל זֶה בָּא עַל הָעֶרְוָה זֶה מַה חָטָא וּמָה אִכְפַּת לוֹ (קהלת ד, א): וְאֵין לָהֶם מְנַחֵם, אֶלָּא (קהלת ד, א): מִיַּד עשְׁקֵיהֶם כֹּחַ, מִיַּד סַנְהֶדְרֵי גְדוֹלָה שֶׁל יִשְׂרָאֵל שֶׁבָּאָה עֲלֵיהֶם מִכֹּחָהּ שֶׁל תּוֹרָה וּמְרַחֲקַתָּן עַל שׁוּם (דברים כג, ג): לֹא יָבֹא מַמְזֵר בִּקְהַל ה'. (קהלת ד, א): וְאֵין לָהֶם מְנַחֵם, אָמַר הַקָּדוֹשׁ בָּרוּךְ הוּא עָלַי לְנַחֲמָן...

Vayikra Rabba 32:8
Another teaching about *"A son of an Israelite woman went out"* — Regarding that which is written *"I returned and saw all of the oppressed"* (Kohelet 4:1), Daniel the Tailor interpreted the verse as referring to *mamzerim*. "The tears of the oppressed," the fathers of these sinned, and these [the children] are shamed, how does it concern them? So too, this one's father committed incest, what is the child's sin, and how does it concern him? "And they have no comforter," rather "their oppressors are empowered" — this refers to Israel's Great Sanhedrin, which comes at them with the power of Torah and pushes them away in the name of "a *mamzer* will not enter the community of the Lord." (Devarim 23:3). "They have no comforter," says The Holy Blessed One: It is on me to comfort them...

I submit, however, that when it comes to the questions of *frum* queer women in *halakha*, there is a wide enough range of opinions to allow for a softer and kinder approach to this question.

B. Practical Implications
Let me begin with a brief restatement of the basic data points:

1. There are two parallel concepts running through all of this literature: *nashim mesolelot* (from the Bavli) and *maaseh Eretz Mitzrayim* (from the Sifra).
2. The Bavli and the majority of Rishonim only talk about *mesolelot*
and do not mention *maaseh Eretz Mitzrayim* (the Sifra).
3. The Rambam subsumes the Bavli under the Sifra, thereby creating
a more robust prohibition.
4. The Tur and Shulchan Aruch basically accepted the Rambam's conflation of the two ideas.
5. While there is a minority that reads the prohibition of the Rambam
(Tur and Shulchan Aruch) as a Torah prohibition, it seems clear
that most understand this to be, at worst, a Rabbinic prohibition.
In fact, the Prisha is prepared to read this as a prohibition about
not being in a procreative relationship.

A substantial group of Achronim understand the Bavli to stand on its own
based on the *mesorah* of Rashi, Tosafot, and the later Rishonei Sefarad. For
them, *mesolelot* refers to marital betrayal. According to these Achronim, the
Bavli does not talk about two unmarried women who engage in intimate
behavior with each other.

This constellation of texts leaves us with a conceptual vacuum regarding
two single women. What does it reflect about the *mesorah* that, according
to this group, the rabbis did not address the possibility of two women,
neither of whom is married to a man, having a physical relationship with
each other?

Here it is important to note that the idea of a person self-identifying as
gay is a modern concept. It may be hard for us to imagine, but for most of
human history, men and women got married and had children even if they
had no attraction to a member of the opposite sex. If they were attracted
to members of the same sex, they might have chosen to "step out" on their
spouse to fulfill their desires, or they might have remained monogamous or
even celibate. Even people who engaged in same-sex intimacy were expected
to marry members of the opposite sex.

Rabbi Eldad Sabag, *shlita,* analyzes both the nature of the physical act of
mesolelot and the scope of the potential prohibition in his commentary on
the Rambam (Hil. Issurei Biah 21:8).[66] He is among the first authors writing in a classic rabbinic idiom who displays awareness of the fact that there

---

[66] באר המלך, published in Haifa 5755 (2014/5) with a *haskama* from Rav Asher Weiss.

are women who are not attracted to men. There were certainly others who knew of gay women, but that knowledge does not appear in the literature. In trying to explain the strange position of the Rivan, Rabbi Sabag writes as a note in small print and square brackets:

ולא מסתבר שהן מזנות תחילה עם משהו זר ואח"כ משמשות, דהא הן
נשאו כביכול אחת לשניה וזה נראה כבגידה באותה "מערכת נישואין"
שהקימו לעצמן. ועוד שכידוע דלפי הטבעים פעמים שנשים אלו אינן
מסוגלות ואין להן תאוה כלל לגבר רק לאשה.

And it does not make sense that they first have illicit rela-tions with a strange man and then they have sex, for behold they are so to speak (*kivyachol*) married to each other and this would appear to be a betrayal in this "marital structure" that they have set up for themselves. And also, it is known that there are times when, by nature, these women are not able [to be attracted by], and have no desire for, men — only for women.

It really was not until the end of the 20th — and for some not until the be-ginning of the 21st — century that *poskim* became aware of the reality of gay women.[67] If we assume that the number of gay people as a percentage of the population has been consistent for some time, this means that for thousands of years, gay men and women were living in marriages that were physically unfulfilling or even repugnant to them. Only in the last 150 years has it even been possible for most people — and certainly all rabbis — to imagine living with a partner of the same sex in a committed monogamous relationship.

In most places in the world, for the vast majority of human history, the idea of two women living together publicly in a partnered relationship was unthinkable, illegal, or simply impossible. Obergefell v. Hodges, the land-

---

[67] The immediate post-World War II climate for the gay community was one of secrecy and discretion. It was not until the late 1960s and particularly the Stonewall riots of 1969 that people began to "come out." At that time, the ethos was one of counter-culture and alternative lifestyles. It is within that framework that we can understand Rav Moshe's strong opposition. However, the Gay Men's Health Crisis, HIV/ AIDS, together with the lesbian baby-boom of the 1980s and 1990s, changed the community in funda-mental ways. The push for civil rights, civil unions, and marriage represents a vastly changed culture from the 1960s. This historical reality once again underscores the fact that the gay community that was known to the *poskim* of the end of the 20th century was fundamentally different from the reality of 2019. Thank you very much to Dr. Kathy Peiss for introducing me to two important works that help to frame my understanding of gay marriage: Chauncey, George *Why Marriage*, Basic Books, New York (2004) and Murray, Heather *Not in This Family*, University of Pennsylvania Press, Philadelphia and Oxford (2010).

mark Supreme Court case that guarantees same-sex couples the right to marry, was decided in June of 2015, just a few years ago!

What can we reasonably expect from rabbis living at the turn of the third century CE or even in 18th-century Prague? Of course they could not have had a well-grounded opinion about two women who want to live together, keep a kosher home, be fully *shomrot* Shabbat and, with God's help, start a family of their own. Such an image, until the last 20 to 30 years, was simply inconceivable to the rabbinic imagination.

I have been blessed to sit with dozens of *frum* queer women who are all seeking an answer to a very basic question: what does God want from them? For too long, and in some settings to this day, gay women have been told that it is their duty to marry men. The first step that I think all communities must take is to stop giving such hurtful and destructive advice. Before we ask any *halakhic* questions, this is a basic issue of human dignity. Would you want your daughter or sister in an unfulfilling relationship? Would you want your son in a relationship with a woman who was never going to be satisfied and would never welcome intimacy with him? Such counsel leads down a path filled with darkness.

Offering advice — both *halakhic* advice and life advice — in an area where we find a vacuum can be very difficult. For many years, people have been filling the vacuum left by Rav Moshe and the Aruch LaNer's reading of Rashi and Tosafot with the Rambam and the Shulchan Aruch. My claim is very simple. It is time to fill that vacuum with a new voice.

The reality of the LGBTQ+ community today is that there is still a lot of promiscuity. There may be good explanations for that behavior, given the history of repression and abuse, and the obstacles in the way of recognizing non-heteronormative monogamous relationships. For those who are trying to live within the Orthodox world, this is not really the case. However, *halakha* also makes claims on people who want to be part of the *frum* world. I agree with Rava that a woman married to a man who steps out on him is behaving inappropriately. When people "hook up" with each other and don't think twice about the implications of that physical interaction, that really is *pritzut*. But when people behave in a way that does not implicate an unknowing spouse and that attempts to maintain *halakha* in all ways, that should no longer be viewed as *pritzut*.

C. *Psak,* Answer:

First, we begin with the understanding that, according to almost all *poskim,* the concern of two women engaging in intimate physical behavior with each other can only be considered a rabbinic violation. That prohibition was expanded by the Rambam, who represents a minority voice among the Rishonim.

Second, the majority position (Rashi, Tosafot, Ramban, Rashba, Ritva, Nimukei Yosef) does not cite *maaseh Eretz Mitzrayim* at all, nor do these authorities refer to the Rambam in any meaningful way. According to this approach, the only concerns, as clearly articulated in the Bavli, are marriageability to priests and licentiousness.

Third, even though the Shulchan Aruch codifies the Rambam's approach, the changed reality of *frum* gay women serves as a push to return to the majority position of the Rishonim.

Finally, the majority position is read by a substantial group of Achronim as referring to a case when at least one of the women is married to a man.

Summary: The Gemara (Shabbat 65a, Yevamot 76a) twice quotes Rav Huna, who claims that *mesolelot* prohibits a woman from marrying a priest (or the high priest), with the express intent of rejecting that position. Rava intervenes and tells us that such behavior between two women — when at least one of them is married to a man (Aruch LaNer, Ishei Yisrael) — cannot really be prohibited but it is, nonetheless, *pritzuta* (licentious). When two women seek to build a Jewish home together, with love and commitment, this can no longer be called (even) *pritzuta*. Rather, given the vacuum left to be filled, this should be understood as *tzniuta* (modesty) and perhaps even *kedushata* (holiness).

Rabbi Zev Farber

Rabbi Jeffrey Fox's basic thesis is, to my mind, clearly correct. Let me briefly restate its essence, as I understand it, in my own words:

Two main sources exist for some prohibition surrounding female-to-female sexual expression.

1. The acts of Egypt (Sifra)—The Midrash on the verse forbidding Israelites from practicing כמעשה ארץ מצרים "like the acts of the land of Egypt" (Leviticus 18:3) states that the problematic Egyptian practices that must not be mimicked are their "irregular" marriage practices, such as male and female homosexual marriage, polyandry, and a man marrying a mother and her daughter.
2. Women who rub (Beit Shammai/Rav Huna)—The Yerushalmi (Gittin 8:3) records a debate between Beit Shammai and Beth Hillel about whether two women who are מסלדות (who rub genitals) with each other may not marry a *kohen*. Beit Shammai forbids and Beit Hillel permits. As *halakha* (almost) always follows Beit Hillel, the Yerushalmi does not lend support to the strict position.

In the Bavli, the strict position is twice recorded in the name of Rav Huna, though it uses the term מסוללות (which becomes the standard term in *halakhic* literature). In b. Yevamot 76a, Rav Huna's position is rejected by Rava, and the Talmud further clarifies that even according to the strict view of Rabbi Elazar, who prohibits women who have had non-marital sex from marrying a *kohen*, woman-to-woman sexuality is just פריצותא בעלמא, "lewd behavior," not a technical violation of זנות, "promiscuous sex." In b. Shabbat 65a, there is a suggestion that Samuel's father, who did not allow his daughters to sleep in the same bed, may have agreed with Rav Huna that this was sinful behavior, but this is dismissed by suggesting an alternative explanation for his rule.

* Rabbi Zev Farber is a Research Fellow at the Shalom Hartman Institute's Kogod Center and the Senior Editor of TheTorah.com. He holds a Ph.D. from Emory University in Jewish Studies, as well as ordination (yoreh yoreh) and advanced ordination (yadin yadin) from Yeshivat Chovevei Torah (YCT) Rabbinical School. He is the author of *Images of Joshua in the Bible and their Reception* (De Gruyter 2016) and the editor of *Halakhic Realities: Collected Essays on Brain Death* (Maggid 2015) and *Halakhic Realities: Collected Essays on Organ Donation* (Maggid 2017).

R. Fox's key point is that the Talmud is either unaware of the Sifra's Midrash or dismisses it, since the discussion of Rav Huna's position is never connected with this Midrash in any way. As Rava dismisses Rav Huna in one *sugya,* and in the second, Rav Huna is brought up but not endorsed, this should have been the end of the matter, *halakhically* speaking, since the Bavli is the main source of normative *halakha.*

What changed in the medieval period is that Rambam decided to adopt the Sifra's Midrash as normative (Sefer HaMitzvot 353) and to conflate Beit Shammai/Rav Huna's position—which the Talmud never explains or justifies with a verse—with the Sifra's *derasha* on Leviticus 18:3 (see Rambam's gloss on m. Sanhedrin 7:4; Mishneh Torah, Sefer Qedushah, Issurei Biah 21:8).

Reading the sources together, Rambam's understanding is that while a woman is not excluded from marrying a *kohen* because of having been *mesolelet*—since Rava dismisses Rav Huna as *halakha*—this is the act declared by the Sifra to be a violation of the prohibition to follow in the ways of Egypt. The act is thus prohibited, and the reason such an act does not forbid her from marrying a *kohen* is because it falls short of penetrative sex, which requires a penis. Even though it is forbidden by the Torah, it comes with no punishment since it is a לאו שבכללות, "a prohibited act that is part of a forbidden category of actions, and not specified in the Torah."

Rambam's take here is unique, R. Fox argues. No authority until Rambam read these sources together, nor is it a likely reading of the Talmud; if the Bavli's authors had been aware of the Sifra's *derasha,* or considered it normative, they would have factored this verse into the two discussions about Rav Huna's position.

If we decouple the sources, to understand the Sifra in its own terms, the *derasha* does not seem to be talking about the sexual act per se. For instance, R. Fox notes, R. Joshua Falk (Prisha, EH 20.11) suggests that the problem is that the Egyptians were avoiding having children by marrying their own sex. According to this interpretation, the *derasha* is not about the act at all (and would be irrelevant nowadays, with the availability of artificial insemination). Even without R. Falk's reading, it seems clear that the Sifra is speaking about marriage and not sexual acts, which is the opposite of Rav Huna, who is speaking about an act that disqualifies a woman from a certain type of marriage.

The question becomes how much weight to give Rambam's *psak,* when it goes against not only other Rishonim and the simple reading of the Talmud, but, in a modern context, turns out to be hurtful to innumerable lesbian women—not to mention bisexual and pansexual women—who are looking for intimate partnership. R. Fox treats this question sensitively and seriously, and advocates for understanding such partnerships as permissible.

While it is true that the act is dismissed by the traditional sources (rabbinic, medieval, and modern) as פריצות, "licentiousness," this is because, until contemporary times, it was taken for granted that only heterosexual partnership was possible. In such a scenario, the act would either be between single women or an act of infidelity. This is clearly no longer relevant to contemporary times, in which monogamous same-sex couples are a norm.

In short, I concur with the above analysis, but I would like to take the opportunity to add two points of my own.

A. Rivan's Position—R. Fox notes that Rabbi Yehudah ben Natan (Rivan), in his commentary on Yevamot, has a different understanding of *mesolelot* than the norm: מטילות שכבת זרע שקבלו מבעליהן "they implant the semen they received from their husbands." Whether this was the full comment or not we don't know since this part of Rivan's commentary on Yevamot was lost, and this gloss was preserved only by the later Tosafot collection.

R. Fox, following the standard interpretation of Rivan, understands his reasoning to be that Rav Huna believed that the sexual act between two women only becomes "real" if semen taken from a man is involved, ostensibly replacing the penetrative penis. In other words, even Rav Huna thought some male penetrative involvement was necessary.

R. Fox then compares this view to that of several Provencal Rishonim who speak about sexual fluid exchange as part of *mesolelot*. For instance, R. Menachem Meiri writes (gloss on Yevamot, ad loc): ר"ל שבאות זו על זו אפילו פלטו זו בזו, "meaning they come on top of each other, even if they eject fluid into each other." Articulating the same idea, Rav Aharon HaKohen writes (Orchot Chayim, Hil. Biot Assurot §27): ועולות זו על זו, ושופכת זרע להדדי "they climb upon one another and eject their seed into each other." Similarly, Rav Avraham min Hahar writes (glosses on Yevamot *ad loc*): מתחממות זו עם זו ושופכין שכבת זרע לה, "they heat up [rubbing] against each other and she [one of the women] ejaculates into her [the other woman]."

Here I will quibble with Rabbi Fox and say that I think the Provencal reading and that of Rivan are unrelated. The Provencal reading makes the following point: even if the women's rubbing of genitals brings them to orgasm, and fluid is ejected from one woman's vagina to another, this still does not count as sex. (R. Fox understands them this way as well.)

Rivan, however, doesn't see the term *mesolelet* as describing a sexual act at all but as an act of spurgling (sperm theft). Rivan's point is that men need to protect their semen from their wives, who can, immediately after coitus, go to another woman—a friend with an impotent husband, let's say—and impregnate her as a favor. Whether or not such a thing was possible or ever happened, the popular myth of the succubus, a female demon that has sex with a man in his sleep and steals his semen—identified as Lilith in Kabbalistic tradition—shows that this was a live fear. If this is what Rivan means, then the whole Bavli discussion around Rav Huna has nothing to do with lesbian activity in his reading.

Of course, this is not the simple meaning of the Bavli, but neither is Rambam's reading. On a *halakhic* level, it at least adds an extra *safek* (doubt) about whether even Rav Huna, whose strict position we do not follow, has anything to say about lesbian sex.

B. Rambam's Method—Rambam's use of the Sifra is part of his overall approach to *halakha*, which differs from other Rishonim. In general, *halakha* derives from the Bavli. Even though, once in a while, a *halakha* from the Yerushalmi (or Tosefta, or Midrash *halakha*, etc.) makes its way into the discourse—most famously, perhaps, not eating matzah on *erev Pesach* referenced in Tosafot (b. Pesachim 99b, s.v. לא יאכל)—as a rule, these sources were not comprehensively included in *halakhic* discourse like the Bavli.

Rambam, however, makes it clear in his introduction to the Mishneh Torah that he will be systematic in including all possible sources of *halakha*, sifting through them, and synthesizing a total approach.

ומשני התלמודים ומן התוספתא ומספרא וספרי ומן התוספתות, מכולם
יתבאר האסור והמותר הטמא והטהור החייב והפטור הכשר והפסול כמו
שהעתיקו איש מפי איש מפי משה רבינו מסיני (מהדורת אור וישועה):

From the two Talmuds, and from the Tosefta, and the Sifra, and Sifri, and from other Toseftot (rabbinic sources)—all of these allow us to determine the forbidden and permitted, the impure and pure, the obligated and exempt, the fit and the unfit, just as sage after sage passed on, going all the way back to Moses at Sinai.

Apparently, Rambam, in contrast to other Rishonim, saw the Sifra as authoritative like the Bavli. Moreover, following his systematic approach, Rambam would naturally try to connect the Sifra's *derasha* and the act described by Rav Huna. That kind of synthesis is what his approach in the Mishneh Torah was all about.

While Rambam's effect on *halakhic* discourse was enormous, given the real life difficulties this *halakha* causes contemporary women with same-sex attraction, it would seem best to turn back to the simple approach of following the Bavli, and thereby jettisoning the idea that the Sifra's *derasha* is normative and that lesbian sex is prohibited.

This is a case in which Rambam's expansive and inclusive view with regard to sources ends up being a burden on many observant Jewish women. Thus, I reiterate my overall agreement with my colleague Rabbi Jeffrey Fox and endorse his conclusion.

Rabbi David Fried

Rabbi David Fried teaches Judaic Studies at the Ramaz Upper School in New York City and is an editor at thelehrhaus.com *.He has semikha from Yeshivat Chovevei Torah and has learned at Yeshivat Har Etzion in Israel.*

I want to express my gratitude to Rabbi Fox for extending to me the opportunity to respond to his article. He is to be given tremendous credit for the effort he put into this topic and his desire to help those who experience pain and suffering as a result of these halakhot. The thoroughness of his research is to be commended, and his actively seeking out responses is a testament to his humility and intellectual integrity. Unfortunately, I believe he makes several errors in his interpretation of the sources and overreads their relevance to his halakhic conclusion. Ultimately, then, his conclusion has no real precedent and is asserted on his own authority. Perhaps if several gedolei haposkim were to concur, it could be accepted, but I suspect this is unlikely to occur as it runs counter to the halakhot and sexual ethics we find in the Rishonim.

Rabbi Fox is certainly right in his assertion that the sugyot in the Bavli can be explained without reference to the Sifra, and that most Rishonim other than the Rambam (and those who quote him directly) did, in fact, interpret the sugyot that way.

One key analytical mistake that Rabbi Fox makes throughout the piece is in taking statements made by various commentaries to explain the rejected opinion of Rav Huna and applying it to the conclusion as well. Rav Huna maintains that נשים מסוללות are forbidden to marry a kohen. Generally speaking, for a woman to be forbidden to marry a kohen, in addition to having a sexual relationship with a man forbidden to her, there must also be a מעשה ביאה. Thus, if a married woman has a sexual relationship with a man who is not her husband, even though this is biblically prohibited sexual behavior,[1] she is still permitted to subsequently marry a kohen if her first husband dies since there was no מעשה ביאה.

Rabbi David Fried teaches Judaic Studies at the Ramaz Upper School in New York City and is an editor at thelehrhaus.com. He has semikha from Yeshivat Chovevei Torah and has learned at Yeshivat Har Etzion in Israel.

[1] Even Ramban, who generally views לא תקרבו as merely a דרבנן prohibition, agrees that with regard to adultery it is דאורייתא. See his glosses on Rambam's ספר המצוות לא תעשה שנג.

All of the commentaries that attempt to pinpoint a specific act to which Rav Huna refers when he uses the phrase נשים מסוללות are not in any way delimiting which behavior is forbidden. Rather, they are trying to pinpoint a specific act that Rav Huna could see as parallel to a מעשה ביאה. When the Gemara makes clear that our rejection of Rav Huna is even according to R. Elazar's opinion, it demonstrates that our rejection of Rav Huna is not because we don't consider a sexual relationship between two women forbidden but rather because there is no act between two women akin to a מעשה ביאה. Thus, the Gemara's conclusion of פריצותא בעלמא would encompass all sexual behaviors between two women,[2] not merely the specific behavior that a particular commentary, in their interpretation of Rav Huna, thought would render the woman forbidden to a kohen. Thus, for instance, Rashi's assertion that Rav Huna is referring specifically to two women who rub their genitals against each other, the Meiri's assertion that they secrete something into each other, or the Rivan's assertion that they secrete their husband's semen into each other, have no bearing on the question of what is forbidden or permitted behavior. They only comment on what Rav Huna might consider sufficiently similar to a מעשה ביאה to render a woman prohibited to marry a kohen.

Of far more interest to us is the question of why a sexual relationship between two women would be forbidden in the first place. It is in response to this question that the Rambam ingeniously brings in the Sifra. While none of the Rishonim Rabbi Fox cites other than the Rambam seem to reference the Sifra, neither do they provide any other explanation for why the relationship would be considered פריצותא, leaving it to the Acharonim to speculate. The fact that the Rambam is the only major Rishon to provide a basis for the prohibition may explain why the Shulchan Aruch rules like the Rambam (besides of course, his general affinity for the Rambam).

The Aruch LaNer's assertion that the prohibition refers specifically to a married woman and the adulterous nature of the relationship is certainly clever, but as we say in rabbinic Hebrew, עיקר חסר מן הספר, such a significant limitation should have been mentioned in the Gemara itself. It is thus no wonder that almost no one else accepts the Aruch LaNer's interpretation, and it would be extremely difficult to build a leniency on this approach.

---

[2] It remains an open question exactly how to define what constitutes a "sexual" behavior. My intent is merely to point out that it would certainly be broader than the specific act a particular commentary identifies in their interpretation of Rav Huna.

The position that Rabbi Fox cites from the Kiryat Melech Rav -- that according to the other Rishonim, פריצותא בעלמא is not a formal prohibition but merely a דבר מכוער -- is not an implausible read. In fact, it may even be supported by the failure of other Rishonim to pinpoint a specific prohibition, d'oraita or d'rabbanan, as the source of the פריצותא classification. The modifier of בעלמא ("merely") might suggest this as well, though it could just mean that the prohibition is not as severe as Rav Huna thought it was. However, even if we accept this to be the simplest pshat, it still cannot serve as precedent for Rabbi Fox's ruling. Besides the fact that the Kiryat Melech Rav nowhere indicates that he would practically be willing to rule against the Rambam, since when are poskim in the business of encouraging people to do a דבר מכוער?

In analyzing the Dibrot Moshe, Rabbi Fox again falls prey to the trap of erroneously applying a statement made in explanation of Rav Huna to the conclusion of the sugya. Rav Moshe's assertion that a woman who has sex with other women has an overactive libido, and is therefore likely to commit adultery with another man as well, was said only to explain why Rav Huna would think she may not marry a kohen (or perhaps only the kohen gadol). It was not said to define why the act is פריצותא (such that we might say that if we know a woman isn't attracted to men at all, it wouldn't count as פריצותא). He comes up with this because, as we have established, פריצותא בעלמא would be insufficient to explain why a woman would be forbidden to marry a kohen. In addition, Rav Moshe, by Rabbi Fox's own admission, is unwilling to depart practically from the Rambam, so once again this cannot serve as precedent.

Furthermore, Rabbi Fox clearly misreads Rav Moshe. He writes, "Rav Moshe goes on to explain that, with two women, it is simply not possible to ever reach the level of a Torah prohibition, because, even for the Rambam, the Torah prohibition is only possible with two people who are considered by the Torah to be in danger of having relations that are arayot." He then quotes a piece from the Dibrot Moshe that supports this understanding. The problem is that if one looks at the entire piece in Dibrot Moshe, it is clear that Rav Moshe articulates the logic for both sides of the debate (whether the Rambam should be understood as a d'oraita or a d'rabbanan) without ever taking sides.[3] The passage Rabbi Fox quotes is explaining one possibility, not

---

[3] Rav Moshe is obviously aware of the well-known debate in the Acharonim about how to understand the Rambam, and that is why he did not want to take sides. While acknowledging that there are obviously gedolei ha'acharonim who disagreed, in my own humble opinion, I cannot possibly understand how

Rav Moshe's conclusion. Ultimately, Rav Moshe is unsure if it is d'oraita or d'rabbanan, but there is no question for him that a prohibition exists. Even if he entertains the possibility that d'oraita there might be no prohibition where it can't lead to a ma'aseh biah, he has no doubt that d'rabbanan there can be such a prohibition.

The Vaya'an David (Dayan Weiss) is of crucial importance to Rabbi Fox's argument because he is the only posek R. Fox quotes who is willing to even consider practical exceptions to the prohibition on nashim mesolelot, allowing it, at least theoretically, באופן צנוע על ידי אשה צנועה.[4] R. Fox wants to equate this case to his case of two women in a committed monogamous relationship, but, if anything, Dayan Weiss seems to be implying the opposite. In context, באופן צנוע על ידי אשה צנועה is clearly referring to a woman who will do this for the other woman in a purely clinical capacity, without any risk of becoming romantically involved with her. Might he be less concerned about the two women being romantically involved if the woman in question was not married to a man? Perhaps, but there is certainly no precedent for it from this teshuva and we have this interpretation only on R. Fox's authority.

What remains is clear. There is no Rishon or Acharon who serves as an obvious precedent for Rabbi Fox's ruling. Even if we were willing to rule against the Rambam (which very few are practically willing to do), it remains within the category of פריצותא. Rabbi Fox's entire psak hinges on his assertion that, "When two women seek to build a Jewish home together, with love and commitment, this can no longer be called (even) pritzut." All of his analysis of Rishonim and Acharonim hide the fact that, on the point where he most needs precedent, he has none.

As I said at the outset, perhaps if several gedolei haposkim were to concur with Rabbi Fox's understanding of pritzut, we could accept it. However, an examination of another case in halakha that closely parallels this one will reveal why I believe this is unlikely to occur. The issue I am referring to is sexual relations between an unmarried man and an unmarried woman. After all, if R. Fox is right that a committed monogamous relationship is sufficient to remove something from the category of pritzut, why should that be true only for two women and not for a man and a woman as well? Like nashim mesolelot, there is a lone opinion (R' Elazar) who thinks that it

---

anyone could say the Rambam doesn't think it's d'oraita. He not only quotes a pasuk, and, unlike the Gemara, the Rambam doesn't generally quotes pesukim as asmachta'ot, but he quotes it in the Sefer Ha-Mitzvot, where as a rule, he only quotes dinim d'oraita.

[4] I have not had time to fully delve into this source and am relying on R. Fox's citation.

would render the woman forbidden from marrying a kohen. Despite ruling against R' Elazar that the woman does not become a zona in the formal sense to render her forbidden to marry a kohen, the Talmud does routinely refer to all sexual behavior outside of the context of kiddushin as בעילת זנות.[5] Again, similar to nashim mesolelot, the opinions on the level of this prohibition run the gamut from Torah prohibition[6] to rabbinic prohibition[7] to דבר מכוער.[8]

The reasoning behind this is laid out by the Rambam at the beginning of Hilchot Ishut. He writes, "Before the giving of the Torah, a man could meet a woman in the marketplace, and if they wanted, he could take her home and have sex with her in private, and she would be his wife. When the Torah was given, Israel was commanded that if a man and woman wanted to marry, he must first betroth her in front of witnesses." The Rambam adds "Before the giving of the Torah, a man could meet a woman in the marketplace, and if they wanted, he could pay her what she wants, have sex with her, and leave her, and this was called a kedeisha. When the Torah was given, kedeisha was prohibited."[9] We see from here two important details about the nature of Jewish marriage: it must be created in a public manner, and one partner cannot simply walk away from the other. For a sexual relationship to be sanctioned by the Torah, there must be kiddushin: the relationship must be created in a formal public ceremony, and there must be a legally enforceable mechanism to ensure that the responsibilities each party has to the other are maintained. Whether one thinks this is a formal lav in the Torah like the Rambam; whether one thinks it is implied from the aseh of kiddushin; or whether one thinks it is a rabbinic prohibition, or merely a דבר מכוער; the basic ethic is the same. A mere stated commitment to each other without any mechanism to enforce it is insufficient to remove a relationship from the

---

[5] See Yevamot 107a, Ketubot 73a, Gittin 81b, et al.
[6] Rambam Ishut 1:4 and Magid Mishneh ad loc., Rabbeinu Yonah Sha'arei Teshuvah 3:94, Shut Ha-Rashba 4:314.
[7] Shut HaRivash 398. (He acknowledges the possibility that it could be d'rabbanan, while seeming to prefer the opinion that it's d'oraita.)
[8] Shut HaRosh 32:13. The Ramban, both in his glosses on the Rambam's Sefer Hamitzvot Shoresh 5 and in the responsa ascribed to the Rashba 284, asserts that a pilegesh is permitted on both a legal and moral level, and does not require kiddushin. This position might actually serve as the best precedent for Rabbi Fox, and the only thing that would remove the pilegesh from the category of פריצות for the Ramban is their subjective commitment to live in a monogamous relationship. The Ramban, however, is an extreme minority opinion. Most other Rishonim believe that a pilegesh is either forbidden on a Torah or Rabbinic level, or else that it requires kiddushin, and is thus irrelevant to our discussion. Rema on Even Ha'ezer 26:1 does quote both opinions about pilegesh without appearing to take sides. Chelkat Mechokek 26:1, however, reflects the consensus of most later poskim that it is forbidden, at least mid'rabbanan.
[9] Hilchot Ishut 1:4.

status of pritzut. As such, I would deem it unlikely that any major posek will endorse a relationship between two women as being not פריצותא, until such time as halakha can find a way to formalize the relationship in a manner akin to קידושין. At present, there does not seem to be any available halakhic mechanism for doing so, and even R. Fox has not suggested otherwise.

One might plausibly suggest that it is worse for a man and a woman because they have the option of kiddushin available to them, and it is specifically the rejection of kiddushin that creates the pritzut. Again, this would be highly speculative and without precedent, though perhaps if several gedolei haposkim were to get on board we could support it. Nevertheless, it would still run counter to the basic idea we find throughout halakha, that changing categories depends on formal halakhic status, not subjective intent. Furthermore, one could equally plausibly argue the opposite, namely that by not giving the option of kiddushin between two women, the Torah was proscribing the possibility of a halakhically legitimate sexual relationship between them. This would be in line with the position of the Magid Mishneh that the mitzvah of kiddushin itself implies that it is the only context in which the Torah recognizes the moral/legal legitimacy of sexual behavior. It is once again clear that there is no precedent to permit, and a decision on this question cannot be made without the guidance of more senior poskim with shoulders broad enough to issue rulings that will be relied upon without clear precedent.

There is no question about the suffering gay people go through as a result of the halakhot surrounding same-sex sexual behavior. But, as R. Fox writes, "There may be instances in which, no matter how much time is spent in the cave, we still cannot find a way to integrate new thinking into the normative boundaries of halakha.)" R. Fox tries valiantly, but ultimately his effort here falls short. We are left with a heavy heart, but as R. Fox writes as well, "We dare not pervert the Torah." Ultimately, we have no choice but to turn to God, who declares, in the piece R. Fox quotes from Vayikra Rabba, "It is on me to comfort them."

Rachael Fried

A Note on Language

Before sharing my response and thoughts on this *teshuva,* I believe it is essential to discuss the language used here. While this may seem like a small detail to some, for others it is the difference between this *teshuva* directly applying to their lives or being completely irrelevant.

Understanding the difference between descriptions and identities is necessary in order to have a productive conversation about LGBTQ individuals. A description is something tangible and objective that can be seen and characterized, and it can include definitions of actions, behaviors, body parts, and more. Identity, on the other hand, cannot be seen. One can only know another person's identity if that person proactively shares it with them, similar to a name. People can have more than one name, they might use different nicknames in different contexts, and they can hate certain versions of their name altogether. The only way to know about someone's name or identity is to ask or to be told by that person.

One cannot know the identity of an individual based on their actions, behaviors, or body parts, and vice versa. A person's behaviors cannot be assumed just based on knowing someone's identity.

It is deeply bothersome when one concludes that any LGBTQ identity is only about a person's sexual activities, desires, or body parts. Conflating identity and the description of bodies and actions sexualizes individuals inappropriately and minimizes identities into desires alone. Each of the letters of the LGBTQIA+ community is about how a person describes themself in their identity and not about who they want to sleep with or how.

There are very few times when descriptions should be used over identity language. One example of such a time is in medical care. There, the anatomy of an individual and the activities in which they engage with their bodies matter. It is respectful for a medical professional to ask about a person's identity, but at the end of the day, it is more important for them to understand

---

Rachael Fried is the Executive Director at JQY, an organization that supports and empowers LGBTQ youth from Orthodox homes. Rachael received her MSW in Community Organizing from Wurzweiler School of Social Work at Yeshiva University, an MFA from Parsons in Transdisciplinary Design, and a BA in Studio Art from Stern College, where she served as president of the Stern student body and a Presidential Fellow. Rachael is a Wexner Field Fellow, a Schusterman ROI Community Member, and a Ruskay Institute alum.

the person's physical being so that they can understand and medically treat their patients accordingly.

Another time when descriptions of bodies and actions apply in a way that they do not apply elsewhere is in *halakha*. *Halakha* is all about actions and, to my understanding, cares very little about how a person identifies. For example, *halakha* is less concerned about whether a person identifies as a kind individual but cares very much about whether that person's actions are in accordance with the *ben adam l'chaveiro mitzvot* (interpersonal commandments) they are given. Examples of this include not speaking *lashon hara*, not cheating in business, not taking revenge, giving *tzedakah*, paying workers on time, taking extra care of widows and orphans, and so on. So too, *halakha* does not care about the queer identity of an individual but the individual's actions.

With that in mind, it seems clear to me that this *teshuva* is about actions and bodies rather than identities. The concept of "*nashim mesolelot*" is concerned with two individuals – both of whom were assigned female at birth and have vulvas – having some kind of sexual interaction with each other. This description can apply to a plethora of identities including (but not limited to) cisgender lesbian women, bisexual cis women, some trans men, nonbinary individuals who were assigned female at birth, women who have sex with women (WSW) who do not identify as queer, and many others. It might not apply to cis women who are on the asexual spectrum, trans women, or a number of other queer-identified folks.

For the sake of including all of the relevant individuals and identities, I use the *halakhic* term "*nashim mesolelot*" as much as possible rather than writing out the more graphic description of the relevant body parts and actions each time I refer to these individuals. Language is limiting, and a shorthand term for this specific interaction with these particular individuals does not feel easily accessible or sufficient.

Assumptions and Generalizations

I once gave a presentation to staff at an all-girls school and asked the audience to articulate the first question that came to their minds when they thought of an LGBTQ Orthodox teen. One brave rabbi slowly raised his hand and answered, "Is he active?"

I appreciated his honesty and suggested we unpack his answer a bit. We were at an all-girls school having a conversation about potentially queer students, and yet the assumption in the room was that we were talking about cis gay men and whether they were sexually active or not. We were supposed to be talking about teenage girls, but we did so through the lens of an adult male interaction.

This way of thinking about queerness is unfortunately more the norm than the exception. In conversations throughout various Orthodox communities, when LGBTQ topics come up, the conversation is almost always framed around cis gay men and their sexual desires or actions. As a person for whom that conversation does not personally apply, I find this framing confusing at best. It never made sense to me that a person could engage in a debate with me about queerness in Orthodoxy while centering an experience that they almost certainly assume has nothing to do with me. Cis gay men are only a fraction of the LGBTQ community, yet *halakhic* conversations almost exclusively revolve around that fraction.

Outside of the social conversations, much of the Torah focuses on men and largely ignores the experience of individuals who are not men. It is a new level of gaslighting to discriminate against a whole community based on something that isn't written in the Torah at all. Two sentences in Vayikra specifically talk about a man lying with a man as he would with a woman. I have considered the fact that I almost wish the *pasuk* did include women so that at least I could be part of the narrative. Instead, women are treated as if the Torah prohibitions apply to them directly when they aren't even written in the story. To me, this represents one of the worst kinds of erasure. Discrimination without true *halakhic* backing is prejudice disguised as Torah, and it weaponizes our Torah.

After exploring the sources, it seems clear to me that sex without a penis involved is not considered *halakhic* sex at all. Because of this, *nashim mesolelot* is considered "mere licentiousness" at worst. I am conflicted about this answer. On the one hand, it is nice for us to permit as many LGBTQ-positive interactions as possible. On the other hand, the reason it isn't clearly *assur* is because it is basically not considered real. This is yet another form of erasure.

It would behoove us to check our assumptions in this dialogue. While the LGBTQ community is one larger community, there is a different *halakhic* conversation to be had around each letter. Focusing on just part of the "G" does everyone a disservice.

Women as Sexual Beings

As a girl growing up in same-sex Orthodox schools and environments, the messaging I received over and over again was that I had to abstain from certain things so as to not inadvertently tempt the men around me. I was taught that girls should not show their elbows, knees, or the separation of their two legs, and they should not sing out loud lest a man be aroused by the sight or sound of them. As a young person, being the rule follower that I am, I obeyed these rules and did what I was told.

As I got older, I wondered why it was that I had to restrict myself in so many ways while the men around me did not. They could show more of their limbs and sing aloud beautifully without reservation. Men playing sports or being loud was even celebrated whereas, for women, the same behaviors were considered immodest. This taught me two important messages about women: 1. Women do not have sexual desires and are not sexual beings. No one has to worry that a woman might be attracted to someone else for the things that they did, said, or wore because those things were simply irrelevant. 2. It is women's responsibility to make sure that men are not inappropriately attracted to them. It was more important to teach me to cover my elbows than it was to teach the men around me to not sexualize women – elbows and all.

Reading this *teshuva* was a new experience for me, one where I finally heard *halakha* acknowledge women's desires as real, important, and relevant. Regarding *nashim mesolelot*, it is said "A man should keep his wife away from this matter. He should stop women who are known to engage in this behavior from coming into his home, and keep his wife from going to them." Some women might have such strong desires, in fact, that it is on the husbands to protect their wives from this uncontrollable lust that their wives might experience. The strong and unruly urge that I was taught exists in all men might also apply to women, and it is men's responsibility to stop that from happening. This is an interesting gender role reversal that *almost* feels progressive in this context.

Rav Moshe Feinstein also acknowledges that there must be at least some women who are sexual beings since he describes *nashim mesolelot* as individuals who have such an incredibly strong sex drive that they must want to have a sexual encounter with every type of person they meet, regardless of gender. Of course, this is considered a bad and shameful quality in women. Meanwhile, as a child I was taught almost this exact same logic about men in a matter-of-fact way with no accompanying stigma.

Rabbi Chaim David Yosef Weiss reinforces this idea in response to a question he received regarding a woman whose husband would not have sex with her. The question asks whether or not she is permitted to be intimate with another woman given that her needs are not met by her husband. His answer is that we should strongly rebuke the husband (as if this will make the husband more likely to want to engage sexually with his wife) and that sexual intimacy between two women is "*pritzus*." He says that this should only be done when there is a great need, in a humble way with a humble woman. Rabbi Weiss then continues on to change his mind in his final sentence, taking back what he wrote in the previous one. It is as if he is saying never mind… this is only hypothetical, and actually it isn't allowed anyway.

Regardless of the outcome, this was the first time I'd heard of some *halakhic* acknowledgment of women having their own desires and interests in other people. In this way, these conversations among the sages feel oddly validating.

Social Norms Versus Halakha
I have long hypothesized that much of the conversation around queerness in *halakha* has grown from a place of societal norms and communal fears more than from *halakha* itself. There are a number of sources in this *teshuva* that further prove this idea for me.

A most fascinating example is the case of an "*androginos*" – a person with both male and female genitalia. This is what is now referred to as an intersex individual. The Intersex Society of North America defines intersex as "a general term used for a variety of conditions in which a person is born with a reproductive or sexual anatomy that doesn't seem to fit the typical definitions of female or male." It is what the "I" in LGBTQIA stands for.

While it may sound uncommon, it is estimated that roughly two percent of the general population is intersex. This is the same percentage of individuals who have red hair. Two percent might sound small, but I would venture to guess that the majority of individuals in the US either know or know of more than one person who has red hair. Seeing a new person with red hair might be noteworthy, but is likely not so uncommon that running into a redhead would cause shock. An intersex person can present with all kinds of gender expressions, including, but not limited to, more traditionally masculine or feminine presentations. It is quite likely that most individuals unknowingly have at least one intersex person in their life.

An intersex individual, according to the Mishnah, can marry a woman but cannot marry a man. The Mishnah is so emphatic on this count that it states that a man who has intercourse with an intersex person should be stoned. The broader topic of intersex individuals, as R. Fox mentions, is outside the scope of this *teshuva*. It is relevant, however, when considering the concept of social norms versus h*alakha* in the case of *nashim mesolelot*. An intersex individual could present as a cis woman or a cis man, and they can *only* marry a woman regardless of how they look on the outside. The idea that a person could present as a woman and only be permitted to marry a woman is quite radical.

It is not uncommon for a person to find out they are intersex later in life. This means that if someone who identifies as a lesbian finds out she is intersex, she can marry a woman *with kiddushin*. Furthermore, but that lesbian individual is forbidden from marrying a man even if she wants to. While this may be the *halakha*, an intersex person who presents as a woman would be more accepted in any Orthodox community if she married a man despite the fact that it may be punishable by stoning. This is because, if we are honest with ourselves, social norms and communal expectations are very strong and can overpower *halakha*. The appearance of a lesbian couple is far more taboo than the appearance of a straight couple, regardless of whether or not their relationship falls within a forbidden category.

In another example, Rashi, Tosafot, and Rishonei Sefarad say that *nashim mesolelot* is only prohibited when the individuals are married to others and engage in this sexual behavior on the side. According to this, *nashim mesolelot* is not about intimacy between two unmarried individuals.

The irony of this delineation is that many rabbis and community leaders promote the idea of gay men and lesbian women marrying each other so that they can be part of the community and live "normal" lives. In these arrangements, it is often understood that those two individuals will have extramarital encounters. There are *shadchanim* (matchmakers) who specifically arrange such relationships despite the fact that they might be even more prohibited than two unmarried women being intimate with one another.

Rabbi Navon is another example of someone who assumes that *"nashim mesolelot"* is not allowed. In fact, he is surprised when he looks in the Torah and finds no such prohibition. It is noteworthy that he assumes this action was not allowed until he could not find anything otherwise. Why would he assume something that he has not seen prohibited is certainly not allowed? And why would he be so shocked when discovering that there is no Torah prohibition?

This is exactly where the Modern Orthodox community is today. Orthodoxy assumes that all queer individuals engaging in any kind of sexual behavior is equal to violating the Torah prohibition, and yet the prohibition is not always there. If we focused more on Torah than we did on communal norms, lesbian women would be treated differently and spoken about in a different way than gay men are. In my experience, almost all queer individuals are discriminated against in the same way, which leads me to believe these prohibitions are based on a social construct and have little to do with actual *halakha*.

I can appreciate that both groups threaten Orthodox systems in a similar way. What does *shomer negiah* mean when we acknowledge that perhaps not everyone identifies as the gender others assume them to be? Or that some people are not romantically interested in the gender that others expect them to be? What happens to *mechitza* and *yichud* and Jewish summer camps? These are all valid questions that we should contemplate, but we can be brave enough to be intellectually honest with ourselves. Orthodoxy has systems built based on these assumptions, and admitting that those foundations might not work for everyone is scary. Feels of fear or threat are very real, but hiding under the cloak of Torah prohibition is not the answer.

Prejudices and Loopholes

Rashi says that the behavior of *nashim mesolelot* "is not the way of the world." I am curious on what that comment is based because it seems possible that it is rooted in a feeling that Rashi had. It is interesting to me that so many men are willing to write so confidently about an issue that does not involve them at all. It is unlikely that these individuals would know what the "way of the world" is, practically speaking, for a population and a private action that does not include them.

Furthermore, Rambam states "that offensive act that happens between women who lie one with the other...it is an abominable act...but has no punishment from the Torah or from the Rabbis." This sounds like he is talking about a behavior that feels offensive and abominable to him but one that isn't explicitly stated anywhere else as such and has no consequences. This sounds more like name-calling based on a general feeling of ickiness (i.e. bias) than anything else.

In the Mishneh Torah, Rambam also says "...even though [*nashim mesolelot*] is forbidden, the court does not give lashes for it, because there is no specific prohibition and there is no actual intercourse. Therefore she is not prohibited from marrying a priest due to *z'nut* and she is not prohibited from [being with] her husband...because there is no [issue of] *z'nut* here. And it is appropriate to hit them with blows of rebellion, since they have committed a violation." This whole paragraph seems to be a contradiction in and of itself: the act itself is not real and therefore there is no violation against it. However, if it happens, it is appropriate to hit them because they have committed a violation. What could they possibly have violated, given that Rambam just said in the previous sentence that no violation occurred?

This again sounds like it is written based on personal bias rather than on any *halakha* or text.

Even in the most right-wing circles, Orthodoxy is a branch of Judaism that relies heavily on creative loopholes. I have always appreciated that the community makes room for innovation within very specific boundaries. My favorite example regards eating meat during the nine days before Tisha B'Av when eating meat is prohibited. Friday night and Shabbat day are exceptions where meat is encouraged, so there are actually only seven days (or fewer, depending on how the days fall out during the week) when eating meat is not allowed. This seems easy enough, especially today when there are so many kosher meat alternatives available to the masses, and yet, Orthodox Jews *must* find a way around this restriction every year. If someone finishes learning a specific set of texts and holds a *siyyum* in celebration, all who are present can eat meat along with them. Many learn for months leading up to the nine days so as to be able to hold a *siyyum* then. Some meat restaurants remain open during those seven days, assuming that there will be numerous celebrations each year so that meat can be eaten.

Similarly, it is prohibited to carry outside the walls of a city on Shabbat, and for this we have a huge loophole: we build an *eruv* (invisible fishing wire fences) in almost every community so that we can carry within those city "walls." It is also prohibited to own *chametz* during *Pesach*, but we've found a way around this as well. Rather than discarding all the *chametz* one owns, one can sell it (or sometimes even sell entire houses that contain *chametz*) to a person who is not Jewish. It is understood that those items will be sold back within hours of the holiday ending, so that people can resume eating their favorite snacks in their homes as they typically would.

These examples continue on in amazing ways. The question that I am left with is this: for whom do we go out of our way to find these loopholes?

The Prisha in Even Haezer discusses marriages between two people who cannot procreate; in his example, these are two cis men or two cis women who marry each other. The problem he sees is that these marriages are not formed for the purposes of procreation. According to the logic of this source, any couple who knows that they cannot procreate (for example, a straight heterosexual couple where the woman has no uterus) would also fall under the same category of prohibited marriages.

Today, two straight people who knowingly cannot procreate can marry without having the stigma that queer couples face in Orthodoxy. There are loopholes for them because the idea of a man and woman getting married, even if not for the sake of procreation, feels "normal" to community leaders and members. Perhaps we are relying on science, which allows for various kinds of procreation for people who have not been able to have children in the past. Notably, this technology is also available to same-sex couples.

So again I ask, who are the people for whom we are finding loopholes and who are the people not afforded that privilege? I believe that pre-existing biases and personal prejudices play a major role in determining the answer to this question. There is a greater willingness to create loopholes for those who are considered more "mainstream," and there is a major barrier for any person or situation who might make Orthodox leadership even slightly uneasy.

Conclusion

I believe that *nashim mesolelot* should be a straightforward loophole for Orthodoxy to find its way around. It is telling that it took this long for a rabbi to formally write about this subject in this way, and I am grateful to Rabbi Fox for taking this leap, knowing it will likely be an unpopular opinion – one that makes other leaders quite uncomfortable.

We jump through hoops to carry on Shabbat and bend over backwards to double wrap our food so we can heat it up in non-kosher ovens. If we can do *halakhic* gymnastics to keep our carbs for the one week we aren't supposed to own them, surely we can figure out a way for *nashim mesolelot* to be dignified members of the community with opportunities for *simcha* and fulfillment.

Rabbi Aryeh Klapper

Introduction

The pain experienced by people who sincerely wish to live in accordance with halakha, and who experience halakha as denying them any hope of a fulfilling sexual relationship, is a primary moral challenge facing the contemporary Orthodox community and its halakhic decisors. We are also accountable for those whose relationship with halakha broke under this stress.

Framing the challenge generically exposes one of the difficulties in addressing it. From an internal halakhic perspective, not all non-cisheterosexual relationships are alike. But from a political and sociological perspective, attempts to make distinctions based on halakha can be seen as avoiding the real issue or as attempting to play one group against the other. Rabbi Jeffrey Fox therefore deserves our gratitude for his courageous willingness to treat lesbian relationships in halakhic isolation.

The opportunity he provides is partially undermined by the parentheses in his paper's coda accusing "too many great rabbanim and poskim" of "viewing Torah through a lens that destroys the lives of gay women (and men)." That coda also risks amplifying a separate chilling effect on halakhic discourse – anyone disagreeing with his halakhic conclusions is presumptively a destroyer of lives, and anyone weakening the social or intellectual force of his arguments is abetting destruction. People reasonably avoid engagement that carries the risk of such accusations.

I don't pretend that Rabbi Fox's rhetoric is a significant contributor to that effect. On the contrary, his willingness to engage in a nominally open-ended halakhic conversation on this issue is another courageous contribution.I therefore feel responsible to engage with his work in the hope that such engagement still has constructive potential and will be received in that spirit.

The best prior *halakhic* discussion of female homosexuality that I'm aware of is in footnotes 13-22 of Rabbi Chaim Rapoport's *Orthodoxy and Homosexuality*. Rabbi Rapoport concludes unequivocally that lesbian sexual

---

Rabbi Aryeh Klapper is Dean of the Center for Modern Torah Leadership and Rosh Beit Midrash of its Summer Beit Midrash program, entering its 27th year of developing male and female Torah leaders. Rabbi Klapper is also cofounder of the Boston Agunah Task Force and author of Divine Will and Human Experience: Explorations of the Halakhic System and Its Values. *He is a popular lecturer who is consulted internationally on issues of Jewish law and whose work is cited regularly by both academic and traditional scholars.*

behavior is forbidden and that the specific behavior of *mesolelot*[1] is Biblically forbidden according to most authorities and rabbinically forbidden according to all others.

The bulk of Rabbi Fox's paper is devoted to expansive presentations of primary and secondary sources that Rabbi Rapoport explained rather telegraphically, and to reweighting or reinterpreting some of those sources. He nonetheless reaches a conclusion diametrically opposed to Rabbi Rapoport's. My evaluation of his argument will therefore rest mostly on whether I find his reweightings and reinterpretations compelling, plausible, or mistaken.

Rabbi Fox's presentations of these sources comprise three arguments for the position that lesbian sexual acts violate at most rabbinic prohibitions. I'll discuss those arguments first, then move to Rabbi Fox's arguments for why those rabbinic prohibitions don't apply to contemporary lesbian couples.

Three Arguments that Lesbian Sexual Acts Violate No Biblical Prohibitions

Argument #1
Let's lay out the key texts as necessary to understand Rabbi Fox's reasoning.

a. Leviticus 18:3 prohibits Jews from acting *like the deeds of the land of Egypt in which you dwelled*. Sifra 8:12:8 identifies four marriages as *deeds of the land of Egypt* that Jews must not imitate: a man to a man, a woman to a woman, a man to a woman and her daughter, and a woman to two men. Since *halakha* doesn't recognize any of these marriages, any attempt by such couples to engage in *kiddushin* is *halakhically* meaningless. The limitation forbidden by Sifra must therefore be a sexual relationship. Sifra thus forbids some or all forms of lesbian sexual relationships as *like the deeds of the land of Egypt*. Possibly the prohibition applies only or especially if the sexual relationship parallels the expectations of *halakhic* marriage, for example if it entails sustained sexual exclusivity.

---

[1] Rashi Yebamot 76a defines *mesolelot* as genital-to-genital rubbing. Tosafot Yevamot 76a cite Rivan, defining it as mutually placing husbands' semen into each other's vaginas. Other versions of Rashi have a combined definition. Rashi Shabbat 65a might have a more expansive definition including mutual arousal without genital contact. Some cited versions of Rivan, and of the combined definition, might refer to women's "seed" rather than semen being secreted into each other's vaginas. Very little of this matters for Rabbi Fox's arguments. I'll point out when something is relevant.

b. The Talmud in two places (Shabbat 65 and Yevamot 76) discusses Rav Huna's statement that the lesbian sexual behavior *mesolelot* makes the women involved ineligible to marry a *kohen*. Rashi on Shabbat 65 understands Rav Huna as making them ineligible only to marry a *kohen gadol*. Tosafot rejects this position of Rashi as incompatible with Yevamot 76.

c. Rambam asserts *mesolelot* is prohibited by the phrase in Leviticus 18:3 *like the deeds of the land of Egypt*. Tur and Shulchan Aruch follow Rambam.

d. Rashi, Tosafot, and the commentators from the school of Ramban do not cite Sifra or Leviticus 18:3 in their discussion of *mesolelot,* or anywhere else in a related context.

e. The failure of Rashi, Tosafot, and the commentators from the school of Ramban to cite Sifra or Leviticus 18:3 indicates that they disagree with Rambam and do not hold that Leviticus 18:3 prohibits *mesolelot.*

Rabbi Fox argues, based on the above, that Rambam is a minority opinion among Rishonim, even an isolated opinion -- "almost the only one."

This argument misses positions that explicitly agree with Rambam and makes too much of the silence of those who don't cite him.

Rambam's position that *mesolelot* is forbidden by Leviticus 18:3 is cited without objection among Rishonim by (at least[2]) Orchot Chaim,[3] Sefer Mitzvot Gedolot,[4] Tur,[5] Etz Chaim l'Rabbeinu Yaakov b'Rabbi Yehudah Chazan MiLondrotz,[6] and Mabit.[7] It is codified by Shulchan Aruch,[8] and no commentator on the standard Shulchan Aruch page or indexed to this *halakha* by the Bar Ilan Responsa Project raises any *halakhic* objection to it. It is also codified by Aruch HaShulchan[9]. I am not aware of any *halakhic* code that rules otherwise or mentions any alternative to Rambam's position.

All the works of Rishonim listed above are mitzvah-lists or *halakhic* compendia. So far as I can tell, no Rishonic commentary on the Talmud either

---

[2] This list excludes Rishonim who cite Sifra but do not explicitly call the lesbian behavior it forbids *mesolelot.*
[3] Hilkhot Issurei Biah 27.
[4] *Lo Taaseh#* 26.
[5] Even HaEzer 20.
[6] Hilkhot Niddah ush'ar Arayot, Chapter 12.
[7] Hilkhot Issurei Biah 21:119.
[8] Even HaEzer 20:2.
[9] Even HaEzer 20:18.

mentions Leviticus 18:3 or engages with Rambam. This is specifically true of Ramban's school, as Rabbi Fox notes.

Rabbi Fox contends that they must all disagree with Rambam. I see this as overreaching.

There are at least four possible explanations for a Rishon's failure to cite an apparently relevant precedent from a source they regard as authoritative:

> a. they might think the precedent is superfluous;
> b. they might be unaware of it;
> c. they might think it is not relevant;
> d. they might disagree with it.

I think option d is generally the least likely. The standard reaction in *halakhic* tradition to a contrary precedent is to cite it and disagree.

Certainly, failure to cite Sifra or Rambam is not by itself evidence of disagreement. One needs to explain why the omission is significant. We'll discuss the proposed explanation below. However, I think the most likely reason that Sifra and Rambam are not cited in the commentaries is that the Talmud never discusses whether the action of *mesolelot* (or any other lesbian activity) is forbidden. Sifra and Rambam are therefore irrelevant for the purposes of commentary.

Shabbat 65a-b and Yevamot 76a cite and discuss Rav Huna's statement that women who are *mesolelot* become ineligible to marry *kohanim*. But there is no necessary connection between the prohibition/permission of the activity and the eligibility/ineligibility of the woman performing the activity. Some sexual behaviors invalidate women for these purposes despite being permitted,[10] and some forbidden sexual behaviors do not invalidate them.[11] So explaining Rav Huna does not require mentioning Sifra or engaging with Rambam.

Therefore, the commentators of Ramban's school may agree with Rambam's understanding of Sifra. Alternatively, they may disagree with Rambam and understand Leviticus 18:3 and Sifra as forbidding lesbian activities other than *mesolelot* or as forbidding *mesolelot* only in the context of a sustained relationship. Or they may see no reference to lesbian behavior in Leviticus 18:3. Their silence tells us nothing.

---

[10] For example marital sex with a *chalal* (son of a kohen and a woman whom he was not permitted to marry).
[11] For example, sex while *niddah*.

Bottom line:

Rambam's *halakhic* position that Leviticus 18:3 forbids the action of *mesolelot* is explicitly assented to by all codifiers among Rishonim and thereafter, as well as several Rishonic mitzvah-lists and *halakhic* compendia. Rabbi Fox does not cite a single Rishon who explicitly disagrees with Rambam's position or mentions any alternative to it. He is therefore incorrect to describe Rambam's position as minority, let alone as isolated.

Argument #2

Rava (Talmud Yevamot 76a) rejects Rav Huna's position that *mesolelot* become invalid to marry *kohanim*. The Talmud[12] explains that this rejection holds even if one accepts the Tanna Rabbi Eliezer's[13] position that non-marital sex with a man whom she could *halakhically* marry invalidates a woman to marry *kohanim*. Even Rabbi Eliezer's position relates only to male partners because women being *mesolelot* is mere licentiousness, *peritzuta be'alma*.

Does the phrase *peritzuta be'alma* tell us anything about whether *mesolelot* is forbidden, biblically or rabbinically? Rabbi Fox correctly suggests that we look at the other two Talmudic passages in which the phrase appears, Gittin 89a and Sotah 26b.

Rava states on Talmud Gittin 89a that a woman's public reputation for having engaged in forbidden sex does not affect her *halakhic* marriageability to *kohanim*[14] because the reputation may stem from people having observed her engaging in *peritzuta be'alma* (and not forbidden sex or an activity that creates a legal presumption of forbidden sex.)

The Talmud then states that Rava's position aligns with a dispute among Rabbi Meir, Rabbi Akiva, and Rabbi Yochanan ben Nuri. Rabbi Meir rules that a wife must be divorced as a presumptive adulteress if she eats, struts, or nurses in the marketplace; Rabbi Akiva says that she need not be divorced "until the women who spin by moonlight converse about her;" Rabbi Yochanan ben Nuri states that since this would lead to an epidemic of divorce, one rather needs "something clear." Rava presumably aligns with Rabbi Yochanan ben Nuri.

---

[12] Or Rava himself.
[13] Some texts have אלעזר rather than אליעזר.
[14] According to Rashi. Other Rishonim think we are discussing an issue of adultery. I see no difference for our purposes.

Rabbi Fox argues that since the behaviors listed by Rabbi Meir are not considered immodest behavior in all contemporary *halakhic* communities, it follows that *pritzuta be'alma* can refer to behaviors that violate socially contingent modesty norms rather than objective *halakhic* rules. Therefore, just as spinning wool in public would (presumably) be permitted nowadays, we can similarly argue that the activity of *mesolelot* should be permitted nowadays, assuming that socially contingent norms have changed in relevant ways.

This argument puzzles me, for three reasons.

First, neither Rava nor the Talmud categorizes the actions listed by Rabbi Meir as *peritzuta be'alma*. Rashi in his explanation of Rava provides two examples of *peritzuta be'alma*, and neither is drawn from Rabbi Meir.

Second, even if we understood Rava to be responding specifically to Rabbi Meir's cases rather than as making an independent statement, that would not be evidence that every prohibition categorized as *peritzuta be'alma* is socially dependent.

Third, the social dependence of Rabbi Meir's cases is about whether these actions that are not intrinsically sexual still carry the implication of promiscuity, not about whether intrinsically sexual actions are permitted.

The other Talmudic use of *peritzuta be'alma* is on Sotah 26b. Rava there interprets a Biblical verse to say that a wife does not become a *sotah* if she violates her husband's demand that she not be intimate with another man "by way of limbs." Abaye responds that "by way of limbs" is *peritzuta be'alma*, and therefore a verse is not needed to exclude it. Rather, Abaye says, the verse is intended to exclude a woman who violates her husband's demand that she not be intimate with another man via "*neshikah*" (=genital-to-genital contact without penetration).

Rabbi Fox contends that "by way of limbs" includes "kissing, mutual masturbation, and oral sex." He adds that, because "the gemara here is referring to actions that might take place in public," "presumably, then, they are imagining kissing and touching each other's bodies."

I do not understand how Rabbi Fox reached the conclusion that kissing is included in sex "by way of limbs." So far as I can, tell this is false. For example, Rambam Issurei Biah 21:1 explicitly distinguishes "by way of limbs" from kissing. In any case, Rambam states there that for a married woman and a man other than her husband to erotically hug or kiss is a biblical offense for which they receive lashes. Therefore, even if one understands "by way of limbs" as referring to kissing, Abaye would still be using the phrase *peritzuta be'alma* to describe an action that is Biblically forbidden[15].

Rabbi Fox cites Keren Orah as stating that *peritzuta be'alma* relates only to the *sotah* issue and does not describe a broader prohibition, and that "the same might be argued in the *sugya* in Yevamot 76a. The use of the phrase '*peritzuta be'alma*' is not intended to refer to a broader prohibition but is only לעניין פסולי חיתון קאמר (was only said with regard to marriage ineligibility)." This apparently suggests to him that Keren Orah does not prohibit *mesolelot*.

If so, Rabbi Fox has gotten Keren Orah exactly backward. Keren Orah was afraid that readers would take *be'alma*, meaning "mere," as implying that there is no biblical prohibition and therefore read the Talmud as rejecting Sifra. He thus explains that the phrase means only that the woman does not become forbidden to her husband. It does not imply that there is no biblical prohibition.

Similarly, saying that *peritzuta be'alma* in Yevamot is only said in reference to marriage ineligibility avoids the implication that the activity described is biblically permitted, thus avoiding a possible conflict with Sifra and Rambam.

Bottom line:
These texts provide no evidence that the use of the term *peritzuta be'alma* on Yevamot 76 means that *mesolelot* do not violate any Biblical prohibition or that the prohibition against *mesolelot* is societally contingent.[16]

Argument #3

Mishnah Yevamot 8:6 discusses an androgyne, a person with both male and female genitalia. For various legal purposes, is an androgyne considered male, female, possibly male and possibly female, or its own category?

Rabbi Shimon and Rabbi Yosei rule that if an androgyne who is a *kohen* married an Israelite woman, she may eat *terumah*. The Mishnah later states anonymously that an androgyne may marry (*nosei*) a woman but not a man.

---

[15] Issurei Biah 21:1. I am not claiming that all Rishonim agree with Rambam about the status of kissing, nor that all texts of the Talmud include the word *be'alma* in all three contexts. But Rabbi Fox provides no evidence that any Rishon understood *peritzuta be'alma* as excluding the possibility of biblical prohibition.
[16] *Peritzuta be'alma* may not relate to the degree and type of prohibition at all; or it may refer to a biblical prohibition, or to a rabbinic prohibition that is not societally contingent; or it may be an umbrella term for a category including multiple levels and types of prohibition.

The wife of a *kohen* is permitted to eat biblical *terumah*. On Talmud Yevamot 81a, Resh Lakish and Rabbi Yochanan dispute whether the position of Rabbi Shimon and Rabbi Yosei applies to biblical or rather only to rabbinic *terumah*. Resh Lakish says that it applies only to rabbinic *terumah*.

Talmud Yevamot 82b challenges Resh Lakish on the basis of the anonymous but undisputed statement in the Mishnah that an androgyne may marry a woman.

Rashi understands the challenge as follows: By forbidding the wife to eat biblical *terumah,* Resh Lakish indicates that the marriage is only valid *post facto.* The Mishnah's language, however, implies that the marriage is permitted *ab initio.* If an androgyne is permitted to marry a woman, then the androgyne must be considered *halakhically* male, so why wouldn't his wife have all the biblical-law privileges of a male *kohen*'s wife?

Tosafot reject Rashi's understanding of the challenge:

אבל אין לפרש
דמדקדק מדשרי לכתחלה לישא
ולא אסרינן ליה לכתחלה מספק נשים המסוללות זו בזו,
דמאחר דמאכיל לר"ל בתרומה בזמן הזה דרבנן
לא מסתבר לאוסרו בתחלה מטעם זה

> One cannot explain this by saying that the challenge is based on a derivation from the Mishnah permitting the marriage *ab initio* and not forbidding it *ab initio* out of doubt of "women *mesolelot* with each other," because since according to Resh Lakish the androgyne "feeds" his wife rabbinic *terumah,* it would not be reasonable for him to forbid the marriage *ab initio* for that reason.

Tosafot therefore explain that the Mishnah's language implies that this marriage has all the legal effects of ordinary marriages, including allowing the wife to eat biblical *terumah*. This directly challenges Resh Lakish.

Tzofnat Paaneiach (R. Yisroel Rosen, the Rogatchover Gaon) explains that Tosafot must hold that *mesolelot* violate only a rabbinic prohibition. Otherwise, why wouldn't it be reasonable to ban the marriage because of the biblical concern of *mesolelot* and nonetheless permit the wife after the fact to risk violating the rabbinic rule against eating rabbinic *terumah*?

Rabbi Avraham min Hahar, who is for some reason not cited either by Rabbi Fox or Rabbi Rapaport, explicitly takes the position that Tzofnat Pa-aneiach attributes to Tosafot. However, no other Rishon mentions *mesolelot* in his commentary.

There are other ways of understanding Tosafot.[17] One might, for example, say that Resh Lakish would not incentivize a marriage he thought was forbidden *ab initio* by permitting the wife to eat rabbinic *terumah*. On that understanding, nothing in Tosafot's discussion relates to our issue.

Tosafot's question also seems to ignore the reality of the androgyne's male genitalia. Even if one forbids lesbian sexual activity as *like the deeds of the land of Egypt*, and even if one thinks an androgyne is or might be considered female, there is no proof that an androgyne and a biological female violate this prohibition via the androgyne's male genitalia. I suspect this is why the other Rishonim don't mention *mesolelot*.

Finally, there are reasons other than Tosafot's for rejecting Rashi's reading of the Talmud's challenge to Resh Lakish.

Rabbi Fox misunderstands Lechem Mishnah, Noda b'Yehudah, and Cheker Halakha as suggesting that Rambam also accepts Tzofnat's Paanei-ach's point and therefore that Rambam must also agree that *mesolelot* are not violating a Biblical prohibition.

Lechem Mishnah, Noda b'Yehudah, and Cheker Halakha do suggest that Rambam adopts Tosafot's explanation of the Talmud's challenge rather than Rashi's. But they do not suggest that Rambam rejected Rashi's approach for the same reason that Tosafot did. Rambam's reasoning, as they reconstruct it, is completely irrelevant to the question of what degree of prohibition *mesolelot* violate.[18]

---

[17] Note that Piskei Tosafot records this Tosafot as ruling like Rava that women *mesolelot* are prohibited to marry a *kohen*!

[18] Explaining what I understand to be Rabbi Fox's error clearly might take several pages, but here is an attempt at doing so briefly. Lechem Mishneh notes that Magid Mishneh understands Rambam as ruling that an androgyne's marriage to a woman is valid only out of doubt, because the androgyne might be considered female, and nonetheless Rambam permits the marriage. This is incompatible with Rashi's explanation of the Talmud's challenge to Resh Lakish, which reads the anonymous Mishnah as stating that the marriage is permitted, and then claims that this disproves Resh Lakish's position that the marriage is valid only out of doubt. Therefore, Lechem Mishneh etc. argue Rambam must understand the challenge as reading the anonymous Mishnah like Tosafot, as saying that the Mishnah's language implies that the wife may eat even biblical *terumah*.

However, the argument that Tosafot holds that *mesolelot* only violate a rabbinic prohibition is not based on Tosafot's explanation of the Talmud's challenge but rather on Tosafot's explanation of why they rejected Rashi's explanation of that challenge. Lechem Mishneh gives Rambam a different motive for rejecting Rashi, and therefore Lechem Mishneh has no implications for Rambam's position regarding *mesolelot*.

Bottom line:

Tosafot Yevamot 82b can plausibly be read as agreeing with Rabbi Avraham Min HaHar that lesbian sex acts, including *mesolelot*, are only rabbinically prohibited. Tzofnat Paaneiach read Tosafot this way.

Note that the argument in Tosafot cuts both ways. Tosafot hold that if one reads the challenge as Rashi does, one must hold that *mesolelot* violate a Biblical prohibition. Rashba and Ritva in fact do read the challenge as Rashi does, and I have not found any Rishon other than Rabbi Avraham Min Hahar who explicitly reads it otherwise. It follows that Rashi and Ritva, who is from the school of Ramban, agree with Rambam that *mesolelot* violate a Biblical prohibition. Using this argument to cast Tosafot as relatively lenient (holding *mesolelot* is rabbinic) therefore further undermines Rabbi Fox's claim that Rambam represents a minority opinion, and especially his claim that the school of Ramban disagreed with Rambam.

Arguments for Complete Permission

So far we've addressed Rabbi Fox's arguments for the possibility that lesbian acts violate only rabbinic prohibitions. These arguments were apparently made on the premise that it is always easier to claim that a law no longer applies because of changed circumstances with regard to rabbinic law rather than biblical law.[19] We'll move now to Rabbi Fox's two arguments for how circumstances have changed and why the law should therefore not apply.

The first argument is grounded in Rav Moshe Feinstein.

Rav Moshe understands the Rishonim as offering two definitions of *mesolelot*. Rashi to Yevamot 76 defines it as genital-to-genital rubbing; Rivan cited by Tosafot Yevamot defines it as exchanging husbands' sperm from vagina to vagina.

a. Working with Rashi's definition, and within Rashi's comment on Shabbat 65 that Rav Huna only invalidated *mesolelot* from marrying the *kohen gadol*, Rav Moshe argues in Dibrot Moshe to Shabbat that this invalidation must only be rabbinic.[20] Why would the rabbis create an additional invalidation? Rav Moshe suggests that the Torah's requirement that the *kohen gadol* only marry a virgin suggests that he should not marry a woman with

---

[19] I do not necessarily endorse that premise, certainly not without carving out exceptions. But this is not the place to discuss the issue at length.

[20] The only biblical requirement for a woman to marry a *kohen gadol* (as opposed to an ordinary *kohen*) is that she be a *betulah*/virgin. Rav Moshe assumes that only a *maaseh biah* can make a woman cease to be a *betulah* and further assumes that a *maaseh biah* is impossible without a male participant.

an overactive libido and that for an unwed woman to be *mesolelet* suggested to Chazal that she had an overactive libido.

b. In a letter to Rabbi Yaakov Breisch, author of Shu"T Chelkat Yaakov, Rav Moshe responds to a claim that Rivan's definition of *mesolelot* forbids artificial insemination by a non-husband donor for married women. His response is that the prohibition of *mesolelot* is categorized as *pritzuta* and therefore does not apply to circumstances where the intent is childbearing and there is no sexual stimulation.[21]

Rabbi Fox suggests that Rav Moshe's explanation of the prohibition of *mesolelot* according to Rivan should also be applied to Rashi's explanation but without the proviso against sexual stimulation. In other words, actions that would otherwise be categorized as forbidden *pritzuta*, such as lesbian genital-to-genital rubbing, should be permitted if done with the intent of childbearing. Because that form of lesbian sex is irrelevant to conception, he further suggests that the requirement of procreative intent should apply to the overall joining of a couple rather than to specific actions. This yields the outcome that lesbian couples who intend to have children are not engaged in *pritzuta*.

This argument takes so many steps beyond what Rav Moshe said that it cannot in any way be given his authority. I will leave it to readers to evaluate its intrinsic merits.

Rabbi Fox's second argument for permission is grounded in Prisha.[22]

Prisha tries to find a common denominator between the four cases that Sifra categorizes as *like the deeds of the land of Egypt*: marriage of one man to another, marriage of one woman to another, marriage of a woman to two men, and marriage of a man to a mother and her daughter. His (to my mind highly implausible) solution is that all of them involve marriages intended for sex without procreation. Thus male and female homosexuality, and two cases where (he claims that) a husband will sleep with a wife but try to avoid impregnating her.

Prisha also suggests that Tur, and perhaps even Rambam and Sifra, regard *mesolelot* as only a rabbinic prohibition, and Leviticus 18:3 as an *asmakhta* for that prohibition. This suggestion seems implausible in light of their clear formulations. For example, Rambam Issurei Biah 21:8 states:

---

[21] Chelkat Yaakov found this argument risible – "דברים כאלו מביאין לידי גיחוך". Deborah Klapper argues that Rav Moshe's logic is incoherent even within Rivan: "There's no conceivable reason for women to do what Rivan describes unless it's to get pregnant."

[22] Rabbi Yehoshua Falk, 1555-1614. Commentary on Tur.

נשים המסוללות זו בזו - אסור
וממעשה מצרים הוא שהוזהרנו עליו
שנאמר כמעשה ארץ מצרים לא תעשו

> Women who are *mesolelot* with each other – this is for-
> bidden and it is from *the actions of Mitzrayim* that we are
> cautioned about this as scripture says: *Like the actions of
> the land of Mitzrayim you must not do.*

Rabbi Fox argues that in our age, when technology allows procreation without sex, Prisha's rationale is no longer a sensible reason to forbid lesbian
marriages, especially if the couple intends to raise children together.[23] (This
argument generates complete permission even within Prisha only if one
identifies the prohibition of *mesolelot* with Leviticus 18:3 and Sifra; otherwise, the prohibition against *mesolelot* may have an entirely different basis.)

Again, I leave it to readers to evaluate this argument on its own merits,
but it self-evidently cannot in any way be given the authority of Prisha.[24]

Bottom Line

Rabbi Fox presents two rationales for saying that lesbian sex in the context
of ambitions to rear children together no longer violates *halakha*, while conceding that it did in the past. These arguments are made by taking rationales
offered by Acharonim for prohibiting lesbian sex and arguing that those
rationales no longer apply. Rabbi Fox does not pretend that the Acharonim
who offered those rationales would agree with him that they no longer apply.

---

[23] Deborah Klapper notes that this logic, applied consistently within Prisha, should also lead to permitting the other three cases. However, Prisha would concede that the other cases are biblically forbidden
by verses other than Leviticus 18:3, and perhaps the other prohibitions have different rationales.

[24] Rabbi Fox additionally quotes an obscure contemporary book of *responsa* regarding the following
case. A married woman has been sexually abandoned by her husband and is experiencing overpowering
sexual urges. She asks whether she can have sex with a woman to quell those urges. The author reports
that he considered permitting her to have a "modest woman" come in once a week to masturbate her
although he ultimately did not permit this. Rabbi Fox seeks to derive from here a position that lesbian
activity is permitted when done in a modest fashion.

Leaving aside the question of whether this source carries any *halakhic* authority, especially within the
Modern Orthodox community, it seems to me most likely that the respondent's logic is that the woman
is otherwise likely to commit adultery to satisfy her sexual urges and that his considered permission was
based on the logic of Sefer Chasidim as cited in Chelkat Mechokek (EH 23;1), which permits a man to
masturbate to ejaculation to relieve sexual pressure when it seems that the likely alternative is adultery
or sex with a woman who is a *niddah*.

Summary: The State of the Argument and the Evidence, and Where We Go from Here

The previous sections established that many Rishonim held like Rambam that the action of *mesolelot* is biblically forbidden. The only known exceptions are Rabbi Avraham min Hahar and Tosafot as read by Tzofnat Paaneiach. This is contrary to Rabbi Fox's assertion that Rambam's position is held by a minority of Rishonim, that he is "almost the only one."

Furthermore, Rabbi Fox cites no precedents among Rishonim or Acharonim for the idea that the prohibition is societally dependent, regardless of whether it is biblical or rabbinic.

Finally, the criteria for assessing relevant social change that Rabbi Fox extracts from Acharonim do not apply to the lesbian couples he seeks to permit.

I reiterate that Rabbi Fox deserves credit for arguing within the frame of normative *halakha*. He might, for example, have argued that past *halakha* simply erred in treating lesbian sex as forbidden, or even as less valuable than heterosexual sex. Or he might have followed Rivan and argued that *mesolelot* means the transfer of husband's semen from one vagina to another and that other lesbian activities are not prohibited at all.

Somewhat less radically, Rabbi Fox might have argued that the need of the hour justifies relying even on an isolated Rishon rather than conceding the need for a majority. As noted in the body of this response, Rabbi Fox cited Tzofnat Paaneiach and other Acharonim who read Tosafot Yevamot 82b as holding that *mesolelot* violate a rabbinic rather than a biblical prohibition. He also cited Prisha's highly implausible claim that Tur and perhaps Rambam agreed. Finally, Rishon Rabbi Avraham min Hahar takes that position explicitly, probably on the grounds that Tzofnat Paaneiach attributes to Tosafot.

Of course, even after making that argument, Rabbi Fox would, in my humble opinion, still need a much stronger *halakhic* argument for eliminating the rabbinic prohibition than his paper presents. He would also have to discount the possibility that Sifra prohibits something other than *mesolelot*, perhaps precisely the sort of marriage-like relationship that he seeks to permit.

The hard truth is that only broadly acceptable *halakhic* arguments can address the pain and needs of people who wish to live in the communities that define themselves by such arguments. Other sorts of arguments will leave them still outside the communities to which they seek to belong.

Coda

There is no obligation to believe that *halakha* as currently practiced and decided is perfect. I support Rabbi Fox's right to assert that current *halakha* regarding lesbian couples is morally wrong and to continue to seek *halakhic* arguments that will convince individuals and communities with *halakhic* authority and integrity to change their practices and decisions. For the reasons set out in the body of this response, I don't believe that his present paper is likely to accomplish this.

However, Rabbi Fox's arguments for complete permission accomplish something very important: they make clear that Orthodoxy currently lacks a coherent articulation or account of a *halakhic* sexual ethic. As Rabbi Fox points out, if we permit and sometimes even encourage married women to become pregnant without sex from men other than their husbands, how can we say that the connection between marriage, sex, and procreation is inviolate?

Many similar questions can be asked – about single mothers, frozen gametes, IVF, and more. Technological advances, *halakhic* compassion, and realism about what restrictions the community will accept have made once-standard claims about the connection of sex to procreation, procreation to sex, procreation to marriage, and marriage to procreation difficult to sustain. What remains is a claim that the connection between marriage and sex is absolute and that the definition of marriage is unchangeable despite all the other changes.

This does not mean that lenient, compassionate decisions on infertility issues etc. are wrong or should be undone.[25] But we need to acknowledge that they have left us in ideological tatters. Until we redevelop a clear, coherent, comprehensive, and compelling account of what *halakha* says about sex and sexuality, the pressure to do anything and everything necessary to relieve immediately visible suffering will intensify, whether or not the advocated-for measures are likely to diminish that suffering.

We also need to acknowledge that for many Orthodox Jews, especially those born in this century, the failure of Orthodox ideology to adequately

---

[25] Although we must acknowledge the possibility that some leniencies will be rolled back, and that this too will have a significant cost in human suffering.

address homosexuality goes well beyond the moral challenge posed by suffering. They simply don't understand why this is an issue.

At the end of the day, I think those who oppose completely permitting lesbian coupling – and on a larger scale, who oppose the complete unwinding of *halakhic* cisheterocentrism -- will need to produce a rationale for prohibition that is intelligible to much of the upcoming Orthodox generation. "*Chokification*"[26] is not a viable strategy here for any length of time.

I don't have such a rationale formulated. But recognizing that my response might make things worse, by obstructing the application of an intellectual fig leaf, I owe at least an attempt at the beginnings of an approach.

Rambam[27] grants that *halakha* may hurt innocent people, more in some times and places than others, just like – the analogy is his – the laws of nature sometimes result in people being injured. He maintains that the job of *halakhists* is to minimize the number and severity of injuries while maintaining the law[28] because loss of the law will cause greater harm than the law causes.

This seems to me the first principle of any viable approach. **It means that we cannot blame the victims of the law. Rather, we must do all we can to mitigate its negative effects on them.**

It is in the nature of Maimonides' framework that the harms of staying the course are often immediately evident whereas the harms of change often manifest in the long term. This is an element of the larger challenge of making good public policy for a broad community while displaying a decent regard for the needs and experiences of those most directly affected.

Granting that some of the *halakhot* regulating sexual behavior directly injure some people, and granting the possibility that they injure more people in our time and place than they had in previous times and places, we must still ask how best to diminish the number of people harmed and the severity of the harms done while maintaining the law.

Rabbi Fox's arguments for permission make no claim that sexual orientation is immutable, nor would they limit the permission to women who reasonably believe that their orientation is exclusively and immutably homosexual. They apply to any woman of any sexual orientation.

---

[26] *Chok*ification refers to the process of relating to a mitzvah previously thought to be rational as instead commanded for no humanly intelligible purpose. See e.g. https://moderntoraleadership.wordpress.com/2015/07/03/chok-mishpat-and-obergefell/comment-page-1/.

[27] Guide 3:34. See also Mishneh Torah Hilkhot Mamrim 2:4.

[28] "Maintaining the law" is a difficult idea. I understand Maimonides to mean both the specific law, conceived of very abstractly, and also the overall structure of legal authority. The two are connected via Plato's idea that any change to the law diminishes its perceived authority.

While Rabbi Fox's specific arguments apply only to ciswomen and lesbianism, I assume[29] that the aspiration is to permit all women and men to choose their romantic partners without regard to physical sex or social gender. I honor his integrity in implicitly acknowledging that no viable *halakhic* arguments for those next steps are available.

Those of us who contend that fully unwinding cisheterocentrism will have dangerous long-term effects must make every effort to gather corroborative data and be open to the possibility of being proven wrong. We are entitled to demand the same of those who disagree with us and to subject claims of short-term harm to rigorous empirical and statistical scrutiny. No serious and honest moral or *halakhic* conversation can take place on this issue unless each side's narrative is challengeable.

My hope is that competing but also complementary urgencies – to mitigate the immediate harms in our times and places caused by *halakha* as currently decided and practiced, and to construct and live with integrity by a sustainable vision of the overall good toward which *halakha* strives – will inspire all of us to do our best Torah work in a genuine effort to convince each other, and that pragmatically useful and spiritually satisfying truths will emerge from a dispute for the sake of Heaven. But we have a very long way to go.

---

[29] See his parenthesis mentioned in my Introduction.

Rabbi Ysoscher Katz

It was a pleasure and *zechut* to read R. Fox's thorough and comprehensive analysis of the *nashim mesolelot sugya* (Yevamot 76a, Shabbat 65a), which is the primary basis for the presumable *halakhic* prohibition of sexual intimacy between two women.

While that Gemara is the primary rabbinic source, there is also the text from Midrash Halakha (Sifra, Acharei Mot parsha 8) that interprets the pasuk (Vayikra 18:3) כמעשה ארץ מצרים אשר ישבתם בה לא תעשו וכמעשה ארץ כנען אשר אני מביא אתכם שמה לא תעשו ובחקתיהם לא תלכו as applying to same-sex intercourse.

R. Fox granularly examines these two texts, *mi'svara u'mi'kra*, textually and conceptually. He explores the various *lomdish* and conceptual angles of these two sources, and at the same time examines the overwhelming majority of observations, comments, and questions raised in the Rishonim and Acharonim on these two foundational texts of the presumed *issur*.

His arguments *le'heteira* in the case of a committed relationship between two women who are naturally inclined toward same-sex attraction are compelling and persuasive. The only obstacle—albeit surmountable—standing in his way, however, is the fact that the Mechaber explicitly prohibits it.

Traditionally, the bar for repudiating a *halakha* codified by the Mechaber is higher than it is for other *poskim*. R. Fox scales that bar with a two-pronged approach. First, he presents a litany of *poskim* who either explicitly or implicitly disagree with the Mechaber's view. Second, he employs the "cultural contingency," arguing that cultural context is significant when determining the eternality of a codified *halakha*. Rav Yosef Karo, z"l, was writing at a time when our understanding of human sexuality was vastly different than it is now. The notion of sexual attraction, and particularly the idea of same-sex attraction, was not a factor when deciding *halakhot* pertaining to sexual matters.

While I left reading the *teshuva* feeling compelled by the arguments and convinced by the conclusion, I can't shake the sense of its overwhelming

Rabbi Ysoscher Katz is the Chair of the Talmud department at Yeshivat Chovevei Torah and the past Senior Rabbi of the Prospect Heights Shul. He studied at the Satmar, Brisk, and Beit Yosef Navaradok yeshivot and has taught Talmud and halakha at a wide array of institutions. In addition, he has directed the Lindenbaum Center for Halakhic Studies, composed responsa on vital contemporary halakhic issues, and writes extensively on matters pertaining to Jewish society for publications including the Forward, Jerusalem Post, Makor Rishon, and the Times of Israel.

audacity. The cost of accepting R. Fox's *psak* is to negate the explicitly stated view of the Tur and Mechaber, and one that is seemingly also accepted by the *nos'ei keilim*. None of the classical *nos'ei keilim* reject the Mechaber's *psak*. Their silence suggests acquiescence.

While the *halakhic* argument is audacious, R. Fox's final words are courageous. Contrasting the term *pritzuta*, used in the *sugya* in reference to two women who engage in sexual intimacy, he writes, "When two women seek to build a Jewish home together, with love and commitment, this can no longer be called (even) *pritzuta*. Rather, given the vacuum to be filled, this should be understood as *tzniuta* (modesty) and perhaps even *kedushata* (holiness)." I couldn't agree more. Queer women's quest for *halakhic* legitimacy is a sacred pursuit.

Lost in this debate is the fact that these discussions are not about identity and personal preference. When members of the queer community turn to Orthodox *poskim* and thought leaders, they are not asking to justify their choices or to provide a green light for the way they live and with whom they partner. That is a forgone conclusion. They are merely turning to us to see if there is room for them in the Torah-true observant community. They want to know if a case can be made that *halakha* is able to embrace their whole selves and treat their hopes, desires, and aspirations the same way it treats those very same feelings among people who identify as straight.

That is a sacred request and something that should be celebrated by those who love and cherish *halakha*. They are pushing us to expand the tent of Torah and widen its doors so that people who have been expelled in the past can be invited back in. Such a pursuit is indeed sacred and praiseworthy.

❧

In the spirit of להגדיל תורה ולהאדירה, I want to add two points to the discussion, one *le'ma'ase* and one merely an ironic observation regarding the development of the various views on this issue.

1) It is important to point out that even if we were not to accept R. Fox's claim and instead adopt the conventional view that there is an across-the-board *issur* for two women to engage in lesbian sex, the prohibition is very limited. Rashi says explicitly that the prohibition only refers to mutual genital-to-genital stimulation. Other Rishonim seem to agree. Meiri defines the word משפשפות as an act that is דרך ביאה, intercourse-like, a term that fits best if we are referring to mutual genital-to-genital stimulation. Similarly, in his Peirush Hamishna, when describing the prohibition of lesbianism,

Rambam uses language that suggests that he too limits the prohibition to one specific act, mutual genital-to-genital stimulation.

Granted, regarding conventional sexual prohibitions, the *pasuk* (Vayikra 18:6) לא תקרבו לגלות ערווה extends the Torah's sexual prohibitions, banning even non-penetrative sexual intimacy. There are numerous Rishonim and Acharonim, however, who believe that the extension introduced by this *pasuk* does not apply to homosexuality. According to them, we apply the concept of אין לך בו אלא חידושו as regards the prohibition of same-sex intimacy. Meaning, only that which is explicitly prohibited is not allowed. Therefore, actual penetration for two men, and the female equivalent for women (mutual genital-to-genital stimulation), is prohibited, but other forms of sexual intimacy are possibly allowed.

2) Many years ago, there was a vehement debate among *poskim* about whether a couple who struggles with infertility is permitted to resort to IVF treatment, whereby she would be inseminated with the semen of someone other than her husband. The primary interlocutors in this debate were Rav Moshe Feinstein, z"l, who permitted it, and the Satmar Rav, Rabbi Yoel Teitelbaum, z"l, who prohibited it.

For those who were opposed, one of the primary sources marshaled for support is our *sugya*, the Gemara that seemingly prohibits sexual intimacy between two women. While most commentators believe that the Gemara is referring to female same-sex intimacy, there is a small cadre of Rishonim (see Tosafot s.v. *Hamesolelot*) who offer an alternative understanding. They believe that the Gemara is referring to women who transfer their husband's semen from their womb to someone else's. The *poskim* who ban artificial insemination believe that this is what the *sugya* of נשים המסוללות is about, and infer from this understanding that transfer of non-spousal semen is, to a degree, a form of adultery.

The unintended outcome of their interpretation is that there is no statement from Chazal addressing sexual intimacy between two women. This, in turn, means that, according to them, it is not prohibited. In other words, according to Rabbi Teitelbaum, z"l, and those who like him thought that artificial insemination is prohibited, there is nothing in Chazal that prevents two women from engaging in sexual intimacy.

P.S. I do have two minor critiques on particular claims made in the *teshuva*. They are, however, minute and technical. I will therefore spare the reader and only share them with R. Fox privately.

Rabbi Aviva Richman

Rabbi Jeff Fox offers a thorough analysis of core sources in the canon from Chazal through Aharonim that bear on the *halakhic* status of the prohibition of female-female sexual intimacy and marriage. This textual analysis is a service to any community invested in the work of ongoing development of *halakha* that is both accountable to the canon and accountable to the lived experience of those committed to living out *halakha*. Many committed to *halakha* assume that all queer relationships are an "abomination" and do not care to pay close attention to the details and complexity of what exists in the *halakhic* canon. In discourses where there has been some engagement with *halakhic* sources (e.g. *teshuvot* recorded in the Conservative movement), often male-male sexuality becomes the focus of analysis. I have not seen the material on female sexuality receive the kind of thorough treatment R. Fox offers in the form of a *teshuva*. What exists includes heavy reliance on the Rambam and Shulchan Aruch in a way that doesn't do full justice to the language found in most Rishonim and many Aharonim.

Specific Contributions of R. Fox's Argument

First I'd like to summarize what I found to be the major contributions from R. Fox's analysis. My goal here is to pull out the most important pieces from his lengthy discussion, in part because the extensive textual analysis he presents out of transparent commitment to the "research" stage of addressing a *halakhic* question somewhat obscures the flow of a direct argument.

1) R. Fox argues for the delineation of two separate origins for the notion of prohibited female-female sexuality and traces their reception history in later *halakha*.

One comes away from the essay with clarity that the Sifra tradition where female-female relationships are considered severely problematic *ke-ma'aseh Eretz Mitzrayim* — "akin to the deeds of the land of Egypt" — does not appear at all in the Bavli, nor do Rishonim draw on this tradition other than the Rambam. For the vast majority of Rishonim, female-female sexuality has

---

Rabbi Aviva Richman is a Rosh Yeshiva at Hadar and has been on the faculty since 2010. A graduate of Oberlin College, she studied in the Pardes Kollel and the Drisha Scholars' Circle and was ordained by Rabbi Danny Landes. She completed a doctorate in Talmud at NYU. Interests include Talmud, halakhah, Midrash and gender, and also a healthy dose of niggunim.

no source in a *d'oraita* prohibition and is instead described by less severe terminology, primarily defined as *pritzut b'alma* — "mere licentiousness."

His intertextual work on the Sifra tradition also suggests that there is some slippage in early *Eretz Yisrael* lists about non-Jews' abominable sexual practices where female-female sexuality is sometimes displaced by bestiality. Though he does not follow this thought fully (it is mostly a brief reference in the notes[1]), it is an important example of how a text-critical lens could be helpful to call into question the solidity of the origins of female-female sexuality being considered a core sexual violation.

All of this serves as a critical counterbalance to contemporary rabbinic voices who have pointed to the Mishneh Torah and Shulchan Aruch and their entrenchment of female-female sexuality as a *d'oraita* violation of *ma'aseh Eretz Mitzrayim* (even as there is no *d'oraita* punishment) without probing the rest of the *halakhic* canon thoroughly.

2) R. Fox sharpens the definition of *mesolelet* and *pritzut,* showing that it should not be obvious that two single women entering into intimate relationship would fall into this *d'rabbanan* prohibition.

Once the relevant *halakhic* category for the Bavli and vast majority of Rishonim is *pritzut*, rather than an *issur d'oraita*, he aims to arrive at a focused definition of what exactly is forbidden. He sharpens the contours of the prohibition in two ways. First, in his thorough analysis of the ways various Rishonim have defined *mesolelet* as *pritzut*, he highlights important contextual aspects of their definitions. Most notably, an early Tosafist posits that the concern is about a woman transferring her husband's seed to another woman (Rivan, p.25-26). Beyond the technical concern of transferring seed, R. Fox stresses that this language indicates an act of marital betrayal (p.26 n24). In this vein, R. Yakov Ettlinger's commentary on the Gemara (Aruch la-Ner) serves as an important Acharon to trace an arc that limits the scope of *mesolelet* to a case where at least one of the women is married to a man (p.44-45). R. Fox stresses that, based on this reading, the Gemara simply never addresses the case of two single women.

Narrowing the interpretation of *mesolelet* does not only appear in the genre of commentary; it is also found in contemporary *psak*, particularly about artificial insemination. R. Yakov Hadas explicitly refers to an interpretation of *mesolelet* that limits it to where a woman is already married to

---

[1] He refers to the phrase לזכר ולבהמה rather than לזכר ולנקבה in three versions of Bereshit Rabbah; see p.11 n7.

a man (p.38 n34). Later R. Fox brings R. Moshe Feinstein's language in a case of artificial insemination, where he states that any concern of *pritzut* does not apply when there is no intention for *pritzut* or *ta-avah* (p.57). R. Fox suggests that these late Acharonim offer precedent for the claim that it is possible to mitigate the concern of *pritzut* in *mesolelet*, especially for the sake of raising children. To be sure, drawing on these interpretations that limit the *issur* of *mesolelet* in cases of artificial insemination requires a formalistic approach that focuses on a narrow view of the technical *issur* rather than considering substantive elements of the case under discussion. It is a leap to go from the context of artificial insemination — where there is no intimate relationship between two women — to the context of two women marrying. Nonetheless, these sources demonstrate that the act of female-female sexuality should not be considered *pritzut* in and of itself. Rather, *pritzut* refers to a context in which there is some other sexual violation — marital betrayal by virtue of entering into sexual intimacy with another woman while already being married to a man — and thus may have no relevance to intimate relationships entered into by two single women.

The second way in which R. Fox argues for a contextual reading of *pritzut* in *mesolelot* is through his argument that *pritzut* in general is a contextually defined category in *halakha*. He brings in other *halakhic* contexts where behaviors defined as *pritzut* become redefined in different historical moments. For example, women eating in the marketplace is considered a *pritzut* violation in the Talmud but no longer falls into that category in our own context. The fact that most *poskim* approach *mesolelet* as a form of *pritzut* (and not as a *d'oraita* prohibition) means that the act of female-female sexuality should not automatically be viewed as *pritzut* but must be considered within the contours of a specific cultural context.

This two-fold approach to narrow the definition and scope of *mesolelet* as a prohibition of *pritzut* lays the groundwork to argue that, in a context where two single women are entering into a framework of monogamous marriage, the expression of sexuality in that marriage would not accurately be defined as *pritzut*.

3) R. Fox argues that it is possible to limit all *halakhic* prohibition on female-female sexuality to specific cases where it is an expression of lack of control over expression of sexual libido and disconnected from building a family, even for the Rambam and Shulchan Aruch.

Even for the Rambam and subsequently Shulchan Aruch, who do refer to the Sifra source on the *d'oraita* prohibition of *ke-maaseh Eretz Mitzrayim*,

R. Fox demonstrates that this should not lead to automatically prohibiting all expressions of female-female sexuality. There is an interpretive pathway that views the marriages in the Sifra as problematic because they are an excessive expression of libido and avoidance of procreation, as articulated by the Prisha (p.40). According to the Prisha, the only way to arrive at a *d'oraita* concern with female-female marriage in the Sifra is to embed it within a clear *d'oraita* sexual taboo, which female-female sex is not. The prohibition becomes reframed as an expression of uncontrollable libido that could lead to severe sexual violation, such as two men marrying, but is not actually a severe violation in and of itself (p.42). In a similar vein, R. Moshe Feinstein uses the language of "excessive libido" (תאוה יתירה) to interpret *maaseh Eretz Mitzrayim* (p.54).

Steps 2 and 3 together provide the basis for a contextual reading of the prohibition on female-female sexuality, according to all Rishonim, including the Rambam. The scope of the prohibition is limited by one or more of the following: (1) women already married to men, (2) uncontrolled expression of sexual libido that indicates likelihood of more severe sexual violation, (3) intentional evasion of the *mitzvah* of procreation. This reinforces the point that there is a lacuna regarding the case of two single women entering into committed marriage to create a family together.

4) R. Fox draws upon androgynous marriage as precedent for how to *halakhically* weigh concerns about female-female sexuality in a context where there is also the *halakhic* importance for a person to be able to marry.

R. Fox's turn to androgynous marriage plays a critical role in his argument because *poskim* there state that, for the sake of being able to marry and build a family, the concerns of *mesolelet* and *maaseh Eretz Mitzrayim* fall away. This analysis allows for a recontextualization of the prohibitions on female-female sexuality for the sake of marriage that is rooted within already existing language in Acharonim instead of what feels like an imposition of present-day values onto classical sources. To be sure, applying these conclusions to the case of two women marrying, rather than androgynous marriage, goes against some of the explicit language in the sources on androgynous marriage where they draw a contrast between androginos marriage and two women marrying (e.g. Magid Mishneh p.77).

Putting all of these pieces together, one can arrive at the conclusion that female-female sexuality in the context of a) two single women b) entering into committed monogamous marriage c) as part of building a family as a *bayit ne'eman b'Yisrael* d) potentially including raising children, does not fall into the *d'oraita* prohibition of *maaseh Eretz Mitzrayim*; does not fall into the definition of *pritzut;* and could even be construed as *kadosh* like heterosexual marriage.

Response: Critique

To the extent that the goal of R. Fox's *teshuva* is to offer a formalistic reading of *halakhic* material wherein the discourse that stresses the *d'oraita* severity of female-female sexuality as *maaseh Eretz Mitzrayim* based on the Rambam and Shulchan Aruch becomes counterbalanced and even eclipsed by many other existing *halakhic* voices so as to create a less severe *issur*, it is a successful piece. Beyond weakening the severity of the prohibition, it also plants the seeds for a stance where female-female sexuality is re-understood contextually so as not to be forbidden at all so long as it is expressed in the form of monogamous committed marriage.

However, the formalistic argument is not entirely satisfying, and a more holistic approach is merely suggestive; the more substantive and constructive parts of the argument are buried and not fully spelled out. In his introduction, R. Fox states that his goal is to "unpack the relevant material...in as objective a manner" as he can, and he waits until the conclusion to offer his own approach (p.5). This leads to a lack of clarity as to what exactly he wants to "unpack" from this material beyond the technical severity of the *issur*. Much of the *teshuva* comes off as a neutral and removed analysis of an array of texts, without clarity as to the overall purpose of the reading. While R. Fox states that taking an "objective" stance is a critical stage of *halakhic* research, my sense was that the essay took this form for too much of the time. Only on p.44 does R. Fox explicitly use the language that one of the sources (R. Yakov Ettlinger, Aruch la-Ner) is "deeply insightful on a human level," the first indication we see that something should drive evaluation of sources beyond objective analysis of the nature and status of an *issur*. As someone who offers *halakhic* guidance frequently, I have no doubt that R. Fox values being "deeply insightful on a human level," but in this *teshuva*, he does not ground his own reading of sources within this framework. Instead, he explicitly foregrounds an attempt to be as "objective" as possible.

When he does articulate his own approach in the conclusion, it feels like an abrupt swerve towards the Aggadic and emotional, not closely connected to the careful analysis of sources he offered throughout. To the extent that his own voice surfaces at a few points earlier in the piece offering a more holistic reading of the sources on a "deeply insightful...human level," it was often terse, parenthetical, and not fully fleshed out. For example, after discussion of behaviors in the Talmud that used to be considered *pritzut* and are no longer treated as such, he suggests the same argument be applied to *mesolelot* and states, "Even though at a certain time and under certain parameters this behavior was unacceptable, that categorization can perhaps shift in a new reality" (p.66). Yet he does not say anything more about what aspects of a new reality would lead to such a shift.

Towards the end of the essay, he makes brief mention of the fact that nowadays two women married to each other can in fact have children through artificial insemination (p.83), but this throwaway line is buried and the implications are not fully spelled out in the context of the sources he discussed earlier that related to the concern of sexual gratification outside of the possibility of having children. Similarly, he devotes half a sentence to state that "the concerns [of *mesolelot*] are made lower in a committed monogamous relationship that seeks to have children" (p.83) without discussing this fully in relation to all of the material he has discussed throughout the piece. In an even more buried fashion, he cites R. David Bigman in a footnote about artificial insemination for a single woman where R. Bigman says that "it never occurred to [Chazal]" that a single woman could become pregnant without a sexual encounter. R. Fox notes that the same language could be applied to the case of two women marrying, "It never could have occurred to Chazal or the Rambam or the Prisha that two *frum* women would want to live together and start their own family" (p.83 n63). Why does R. Fox leave this comment to one footnote? Isn't this exactly where the creative application of source material needs to be done, drawing explicitly on precedents in our contemporary moment and discussing at length how the arguments there are or are not relevant to the case of two women getting married?

R. Fox clearly thinks that something has changed in how to approach sexuality and marriage in contemporary times but does not get into what he means. Is he referring to shifting understandings of sexuality within Modern Orthodox feminist Jewish communities? Is he referring to widespread acceptance of LGBTQ marriage in the United States of America, which, to be sure, is not a unanimous cultural reality? If he is referring to a wider American approach to sexuality, why wouldn't that be considered external to Jewish culture as *maaseh Eretz Mitzrayim*? What are the Torah sources and values that he sees as driving a "new reality" that would affect the way our interpretation of *halakha* should approach two women marrying? He leaves all of this up to the reader, and I find this to be the most important lack in the piece. One is left with a bit of the feeling עיקר חסר מן הספר — that the main work that needs to be done is not here.

I wonder if part of the motivation for leaving these kinds of comments as parenthetical and buried has to do with his desire to differentiate his analysis from other existing modes of *halakhic* discussion on this topic and other topics related to gender and sexuality. The kind of historical argument to which he very vaguely alludes has been made – and at greater length – in some of the *responsa* of the Conservative movement, though without the rigorous and thorough analysis of Rishonim and Aharonim that R. Fox offers. One gets the sense that R. Fox wants to present a different form of discourse by staying within sources of the *halakhic* canon, but his assumptions about how these texts approached marriage and sexuality, and how this differs from his own approach, are then not stated explicitly. It is also important to be aware of responses to these kinds of historical arguments within the Conservative movement where this issue has been discussed at greater length. For example, R. Joel Roth, in his 2006 essay, makes some reference to recent academic work about models of same-sex relationships in late antiquity, which he believes debunks the notion that Chazal couldn't imagine same-sex consensual partnerships. All of this is to say that R. Fox's lack of engagement with the history of sexuality leads to somewhat sloppy assumptions about earlier sources and how they approached sexuality.[2] To the extent that one wants to engage in a contextual reading of earlier sources, historical scholarship should not be ignored just because it has been deployed in non-Orthodox settings. *Aderaba* – it would be incredibly valuable to integrate these sources within the robust normative discussion of Rishonim and Aharonim that R. Fox offers.

Beyond the buried arguments and sloppiness about historical understandings of sexuality, a major concern I have about this *teshuva* is the overall framing. Once the question begins from assuming that there is a prohibition of female-female sexuality and then tries to ascertain the "objective" level of severity of that *issur*, there is already a losing battle for the subjectivity of someone who identifies as lesbian who wants to understand her place within *halakha*. The framing here assumes that female-female sexuality is a problem and then focuses on how much of a problem it is. I

---

[2] Another example is his discussion of the Rivan and others that deal with female seed, where he does not fully explore how these Rishonim understood the nature of female secretions and their status in terms of *zera*. See Tirzah Meacham, *Nashim lav b'not hargashah ninhu* in *A Woman and her Judaism: A Contemporary Religious-Feminist Discourse* ed. Tova Cohen (Jerusalem: Rubin Mass, 2013), pp. 153-174.

wonder how the process of *halakhic* research and writing can itself place the questioner's subjectivity front and center, and contribute to their sense of being within the *halakhic* conversation rather than being discussed as a marginal case and a "problem." I would hope that anyone who asks a *halakhic* question about their sexuality could expect that the response not primarily be about solving a *halakhic* problem that ideally would not exist. Instead, their sincere *halakhic* question should become a locus for more deeply understanding the intersection between *halakha,* sexuality and marriage, both for the individual and for the *halakhic* community writ large. A response focused on objectively trying to determine "how forbidden" female-female sexuality is will not do that work. The framing must get much more deeply into the substantive issues animating the case in question.

Perhaps the most important (but also somewhat buried) conclusion R. Fox offers in this regard is that the Talmud, and the entire *halakhic* canon based on it, is not speaking to two single women and only addresses female-female sexuality when it is within the framework of marriage to a man. It speaks to men, not to women. Mostly it speaks to husbands who have concerns about their wives' sexuality.[3] In some ways, this lacuna is freeing: it eliminates the applicability of the *halakhic* prohibition in the case of two single women who want to get married. In other ways, it is devastating: the message to the lesbian woman is that *halakha* does not see her; it is not speaking to her reality. The only way to view her sexuality and marriage without the assumption that it is "problematic" is to conclude that it is entirely off the radar of *halakha*. This hardly leads to a sense of a religiously grounded approach towards sexuality, marriage and family for two women whose lives are otherwise fully anchored within *halakha*.

As opposed to an analysis that leads to a sense of being totally out of the canon, an approach to same-sex sexuality based on left-handedness articulated by my colleague and teacher R. Ethan Tucker leaves room for the heterosexually-focused *halakhic* discourse on sexuality to remain alive, albeit with the need for translation into one's own "orientation." Much of what Talmud and *halakha* have to say about practices rooted in right-handedness (e.g. laying *tefillin*) is still applicable to someone who is left-handed but requires an act of translation. So too, two women entering into marriage would inherit and be guided by Torah and *halakha*'s approach to sexuality, including the substantive concerns behind *ma-aseh*

---

[3] With the exception of Avuha d'Shmuel (Shabbat 65a, p.15), a father concerned about his daughters' sexuality.

Eretz Mitzrayim and *pritzut*, while translating these concerns into a different sexual orientation.

Or, as opposed to positing direct translation through the left-handed framework, one might articulate substantive arguments for why female-female sexuality does NOT share some of the concerns relevant to *halakha's* concern with male sexual violation. The existence of a *halakhic* lacuna about two single women engaging in female-female sexuality may indicate that substantive concerns rooted in penile penetrative intercourse are entirely different. Being free from sexual prohibitions rooted in a male-centered discourse of *halakha* would then require articulating the substantive differences of female-female sexuality.

R. Fox does not really take either of these substantive paths. His framing suggests that drawing the lines of *issur* so that *halakha* simply doesn't include two single women marrying each other is a blessed lacuna. This formalist approach ultimately suggests that there is value in being "freed" from having to interface with *halakha*. It hardly feels like a robust approach to a life of engaging with and living out a religious vision rooted in *halakha*.

Response: Alternative Framing

As an alternative framing, I would bring to the surface aspects of the *halakhic* texts quoted that could center the subjecthood of lesbian women seeking how Torah and *halakha* speak to their experience and choices around sexuality, marriage, and family.

To what extent do these sources take female sexuality seriously as a legitimate desire that should have an *halakhically* valid outlet for expression and simultaneously needs to be constrained and channeled through religious piety, just as is the case in heterosexuality? If we conclude that the *halakhic* interpretation with the most integrity does not define female-female sexuality in monogamous marriage as *pritzut* but rather as the proper outlet for sexuality for these individuals, then we must also be able to clearly define what *pritzut* is. Taking lesbian women seriously as *halakhic* actors involves both of these steps, not just the stance of "discovering a *kula* (leniency)" by showing that the prohibition of *mesolelet* doesn't apply to them. Being "freed" from a prohibition in a way that also robs them of a canon that speaks to their experience is not particularly religiously meaningful.

It does a disservice to *halakha* and to religious people's experience to approach the material and analysis R. Fox brings to the table merely as the discovery of a *kula* (leniency) that establishes freedom from an *halakhic* stricture such that *halakha* has no more to say about female-female sexuality. The content surfaced through his analysis brings to our attention many fundamental aspects about the nature of sexuality and partnership that can be a source of learning for all Jews. When is sexual behavior *pritzut* and when is it *tzniut*? What kinds of sexual relationships are a *toevah* and why? What *halakhic* sources speak to the importance for everyone to have the option to pursue meaningful sexual intimacy and raise children in the context of a partnership that is conducive to happiness?

As an example of centering the importance of a woman's sexual fulfillment, the teshuvah of R. Chaim Dovid Yosef Weiss (p.59-60) is really the first source R. Fox brings where a woman poses a *halakhic* question about her experience of sexuality, as her husband is sexually neglecting her and the mitzvah of *onah*. R. Fox focuses on the technical way in which R. Weiss treats the status of the prohibition of *mesolelet* but says very little about the significance of the fact that this source centers female subjectivity in the *halakhic* canon. As one bullet point on a list, R. Fox notes that R. Weiss "understands the need for sexual fulfillment to be significant within the *halakhic* process," but R. Fox does not linger on this point more fully. For a lesbian woman wondering about *halakhic* contours for expressing sexuality, this is a significant moment. Instead of a religious pathway coming from being absent in the text (the Gemara never imagined two women getting married), the religious pathway comes from being seen in the text (R. Weiss acknowledges the *halakhic* importance of sexual satisfaction for women and that this might be fulfilled with another woman).

Along these lines, I would center a more holistic *halakhic* approach by asking the following questions that center a lesbian woman's experience and perspective: What sources in *halakha* address the importance that women be able to enter into marriage that is conducive to happiness and to creating the context for a positive relationship to Torah, *mitzvot*, and Hashem? Can we reinterpret and move beyond language that is centered around the male imperative to marry and have children so as to clarify how these imperatives apply to women? What language do we find about the importance for individuals to have/raise Jewish children in a context that will be embedded in love and care rather than deceit and frustration (which can arise if someone not attracted to a man thinks their only option is heterosexual marriage)?

These questions could frame an approach to many of the sources R. Fox brings that is more holistic than the narrow question of the status of the *issur* of *mesolelet*. But these questions may also require drawing upon sources with a less narrow lens, expanding the scope of research beyond sources that deal directly with the prohibition of *mesolelet.*

As one example of a first-person attempt where someone who identifies as lesbian and *halakhically* observant shares her quest through a number of *halakhic* sources (including many that R. Fox brings) it is worthwhile to consider the essay by Ziva Ofek on the website of Bat Kol, an Israeli organization for lesbian women who are also *halakhically* observant. Ofek spends a significant part of her discussion on the importance of partnership, including sources that explicitly address the importance of partnership for a woman and not just for a man (as is presumed in most *halakhic* discourse and codified in the Shulchan Aruch Even ha-Ezer 1:1).

R. Fox brings some sources that relate to this more expansive lens, for example drawing on the discussion of artificial insemination for a single woman, but does not fully bring this to bear on larger questions about the *halakhic* importance that all women have an outlet to have children. Some of the sources related to artificial insemination intersect with questions relevant to same-sex marriage for women, as both relate to the issue of *halakhic* pathways to have children for someone for whom heterosexual marriage is not an option. What is the *halakhic* value of a woman having children: is it a mitzvah or is it entirely *reshut* (optional)? What language do *halakhic* sources offer about the importance of partnership for raising children or the importance of the emotional wellbeing of a parent? *Halakhic* discussion about single women having children might be aligned with, but might be in tension with, the *halakhic* framing of two women marrying to raise a family. By leaning into the substantive issues underlying these various questions, we should learn more about the nature of *halakha* and bodily autonomy, and the multiplicity of *halakhic* pathways to create family.

As an example of how to approach these sources for a more substantive and less technical treatment of the prohibition of *mesolelet,* one could build upon R. Fox's analysis of the root סלל so as to more clearly develop the nature of sexual activity that is considered *halakhically* problematic. R. Fox brings a plethora of definitions and explanations of the term, but he does not fully explore what is at stake in various definitions. This leaves the reader with a sense of uncertainty as to what is gained from all the definitions. As a reader, I would even say that, without that clarity of purpose and framing, there is a danger for this kind of collection of sources to feel a bit voyeuristic or even like an act of *pritzut* in and of itself. Without a clear sense of purpose as to what we are looking for that has important *halakhic* significance, it feels like a violation of privacy to be so closely engaging with and picturing the mechanics of female-female sex acts. The discomfort is amplified by virtue of the fact that this is a discussion by a man based on texts authored by male *poskim* from across the centuries about women's sexual behaviors. One is left to wonder if part of the existence of this material defining female-female sexuality over the centuries has served as a site for male fantasy. I do not at all suggest that this is an intended purpose, but it can be an effect of the style of listing so many definitions without a clear goal of what is to be gained from these definitions.

I would suggest that this array of definitions of *mesolelet* could more effectively be aimed at trying to understand what exactly may be considered *halakhically* problematic about this behavior, particularly along the lines of objectification. R. Fox brings Midrash Sechel Tov, which explains *mesolelet* as "rubbing up against a wall," (p.23) and he notes an intertext in Mishnah Bava Kamma 4:6 that deals with an ox rubbing up against a wall (p.23 n20). Yet, he does not make any reference to the way in which this intertext very explicitly introduces objectification, which may point to a valence of *mesolelet* that is about using another person as an object for one's own sexual gratification. In light of this objectifying intertext, one might interpret the accusation of how Pharoah treats Israel (עודך מסתולל בעמי) as essentially "playing" with Israel – or, to be more graphic, Pharoah using Israel as an object for a kind of political "masturbation," using Israel as an object for his own gratification. Once we see this valence in the meaning of *mesolelet,* it makes sense to differentiate the woman who is a *mesolelet* using her young male child as another example of objectification, that is, using someone else across a power divide for one's own gratification. Even if this technically may not disqualify her vis-a-vis the *kehuna*, it should certainly still be considered *halakhically* problematic as *pritzut*. One problematic aspect of *pritzut* might then be understood as using someone else as an object for sexual gratification, especially across power differentials. In this vein, we could sharpen the problem of women who are already married to men and are *mesolelot* with each other as not only an act of marital betrayal against their husbands and/or "excessive" libido but also as a problem of objectifying someone else for sexual gratification outside of a clear context of a committed relationship. This meaning of *pritzut* could help sharpen our understanding of a dimension that can be problematic in any sexual encounter, not limited to the case of two women and *mesolelot*.

CONCLUSION

In some ways, the most important work R. Fox does in this essay is to over-come a first hurdle for more holistic *halakhic* engagement about two women marrying by limiting concerns about the *issur* of *mesolelot*. He points us in the direction of needing to clarify the substantive issues that may stand behind the many sources that have defined certain expressions of female-fe-male sexuality as *pritzut*. Yet, ultimately, I would suggest that the stance isn't about looking at something "problematic" *halakhically* and trying to figure out how to minimize the "problem." A "minimize the problem" stance assumes that it would be much better not to have to address the problem at all. But it is hardly dignifying for someone to have to view their sexual expression, partnership, and family as *bedieved* — essentially a problem, no matter how big or small.

Once R. Fox has engaged in *halakhic* "damage control," correcting for what he sees as misconceptions of the force and nature of the *issur* of *me-solelet* that have led to much harm and frustration, it may be more possible to open the floodgates of a rich exploration of how female-female sexuality contributes to our larger understanding of sexuality and partnership in *halakha*. That next stage would lead with the following questions:

To what extent do the people asking questions about female-female sex-uality based in their own lives feel seen by *halakhic* analyses? Is there lan-guage in the sources – and/or in the discussion of the sources – that feels like it understands their experiences, feelings, and real questions? Do they themselves feel they can step into this conversation, cast their own gaze onto the *halakhic* sources, and find deeper meaning in Torah and in their lives based on this encounter? Are they part of an approach to *halakha* that is accountable to defining what ARE considered substantive contours of sexual violation – *maaseh Eretz Mitzrayim* and *pritzut* – even as their own marriage may not fall within those understandings?

Finally, one critical question in imagining two single women entering into *halakhic* marriage is the following: Is it possible to go from a stance of "problem" and *pritzut* to something that is actually a blessing? In this vein, there is a powerful midrash about Sarah Immenu nursing in public so as to make known the divine miracle of giving birth to Yitzhak in her old age. The midrash explains that she was hesitant to violate a *pritzut* norm (indeed, nursing in public is one example R. Fox mentions that has been defined as *pritzut* in earlier sources, Gittin 89a, p.65). The midrash has Avraham reassure her that this is not the time to be "modest." Doing an action that she thinks of as *pritzut* is actually the way to sanctify God's name in this moment:

...והיה אבינו אברהם או' לשרה, שרה אין זו שעה של הצניע, קדשי
שמו של הקדוש ברוך הוא ושבי בשוק והניקי בניהם...(פסיקתא דרב
כהנא (מנדלבוים) פיסקא כב - שוש אשיש)

> ...Avraham Avinu said to Sarah: Sarah this is not the time for modesty! Sanctify the Holy Blessed One's name and sit in the marketplace and nurse their children!..(Pesikta de-Rav Kahana Piska 22 *Sos A-sis*)

The Aggadic genre of this story may not be immediately applicable to *halakhic psak*, and the case of nursing in public is arguably very different from female-female sexuality – even though both are technically defined as *pritzut*. Nonetheless, this midrash speaks to the tentativeness that can arise around a behavior one has been taught to think is *pritzut* and how failure to understand the reality of the moment might mean that one misses out on *kiddush Hashem*. When I see a reality of *frum* women living in partnership and building homes and families dedicated to Torah and *mitzvot*, these words of Avraham resonate strongly: now is not the time to "be modest" and assume that the most pious pathway is to suppress a behavior that people have construed as *pritzut*. If we can see clearly and are not stuck in misconceptions about the nature of *pritzut*, we are poised to create the possibility for a *kiddush Hashem*. A *posek* — like Avraham Avinu — can be in the position of encouraging someone to see past their fears and anxieties so as to live out a life that is a *kiddush Hashem*.

There is a delicate dance between the role of a *posek* as ally who helps establish trust in the *halakhic* system and the role of a person who has a particular identity getting to be in the driver's seat as the full subject who sifts through *halakha* seeing what they find resonant for themselves. Sometimes people with a marginal identity need someone else who feels more comfortable and with expertise inside *halakhic* material to get into the trenches and do the interpretive work so that they can trust that it is possible to engage *halakha* at all. But there are also limits to what an external view can bring to the table. Some of the most creative work about female-female sexuality in *halakha* will likely emerge as women who are attracted to women do their own meaning-making and trace the pathways that feel most accountable to *halakha* and to their lives. For this work to continue to unfold, R. Fox in his life's work offers an invaluable contribution as someone who teaches *halakha* to women towards *semikha*. In ongoing *havruta,* may their *beit midrash* continue to be fertile ground for ripening *chiddushim* related to gender and sexuality in addition to many other areas of *halakha.*

Miryam Kabakov

The presumption that undergirds any new *p'sak halakha* or *teshuva* is that someone out there is seeking answers. There are no *teshuvot* without people bringing *she'elot*. In "Gay Women (Nashim Mesolelot): A Teshuva," Rabbi Fox seeks to answer the questions: Is a specific sexual act between two women permissible? To what extent, if any, is sexual contact between women forbidden under Jewish law?

But who is asking this question? Who exactly is waiting for a solution to a *halakhic* problem? The absence of a *sho'el/et*, a questioner, to whom this *teshuva* is addressed points directly to the fact that the *implied* questioners have already given themselves the answer. Modern Orthodox lesbians are, generally speaking, not asking permission simply to exist as themselves these days. That is because frum women have been finding each other in community for decades now, making coming out immeasurably easier for women today. They have no need for pages of Talmudic precedent to prove that their sexual identities are legitimate.

Noticing this absence, hearing the silence where the voice of a *sho'el/ et* should be, enables us to appreciate for whom the strictly *halakhic* arguments of "Gay Women (Nashim Mesolelot): A Teshuva" is written: people with *intellectual* rather than *existential* questions. I learned the difference between these modes of approaching the text thanks to a life I have lived not only in relationship with Torah and *halakha*, but in relationship with other learned Jewish lesbians, for whom the texts of our tradition have been a part – but not the only part – of a lifelong quest to make Orthodoxy hospitable for LGBTQ+ Jews.

When I was in my 20s, a group of queer Jewish women in Israel welcomed me into their circle. All of them had once thought, like me, that we were the only ones of our kind. After we found each other and formed a social group, we likewise were sure that this group was the only one of its kind. When Shavuot came, we decided to devote the entire night to learning whatever sources we could find about lesbians in the Torah, Talmud and recent rabbinic literature and responsa. One of our members was a Torah scholar, well known in *frum* circles for her wide breadth of Torah knowledge. She had been married several times to men, but her repeated attempts

Miryam Kabakov is a founder and Executive Director of Eshel, a support, education, and advocacy organization for LGBTQ+ Orthodox Jews. She is the editor of the anthology Keep Your Wives Away From Them: Orthodox Women, Unorthodox Desires *(2010, North Atlantic Books).*

to live a heterosexual life didn't work. That Shavuot, she taught us every text that mentioned women attracted to women in the rabbinic sources. She unearthed all of the texts *hazal* had ever written about lesbians and she taught them to the weave of women who gathered that night.

The most exciting passage we learned was a passage from Rambam's *Mishneh Torah* (*Sefer Kiddushah, Hilchot Issurei Bi'ah* 21:8). Here, Rambam brings two distinct perspectives on what "lesbians" (in today's terms) are: he pairs the Talmud's understanding that there are women who have sexual relationships with one another –

nashim mesolelot zoh b'zoh – with the Sifra's recognition of marriage between two women as one of the *ma'aseh mitzrayim* that we are commanded not to do. Rambam's innovation was to bring these two distinct categories together, attaching a lesbian sexual act to the social category of marriage. Finally! we thought. Someone got it! Rambam understood, as the Talmud and earlier *midrashic* literature did not, that being gay had a sexual *and* a social dimension; our lives are defined not just by whom we desire but with whom we want to build a life. But this very understanding meant that Rambam was pointing an accusatory finger directly at us. *We* were the women the Rambam was describing as dangerous and licentious. *We* were the ones from whom, he warned his (presumably male, heterosexual) readers, they should keep their wives away.

Learning this source could have demoralized us. But that's not what happened. The power of learning Rambam and all the other texts was, in fact, overwhelmingly positive. Why? In part, because our learning showed us that the rabbinic tradition recognized our existence. For a moment, we were no longer invisible in the Jewish communities of the past, even if we were often unseen in our Orthodox communities. But more than that, it was because we learned these sources together, as proud Orthodox Jewish lesbian women. As such, we knew that we were more than those categories. Even if the rabbis of the past knew us only for a sexual act or a sexual identity, or condemned us for being who we were, we affirmed *for each other* that we were whole people. By bringing our whole selves to the act of studying Torah together, we could see that the texts hold up a very partial mirror. After learning the sources that Shavuot, we laughingly adopted the moniker "*nashim mesolelot*" for ourselves. We claimed it ironically and a bit proudly, feeling that the sages of our tradition had glimpsed us just a bit and knowing there was so much more to us than what they saw. (Elaine Chapnik captures the sources' complexity – and the ultimately empowering experience of our study of them – in her essay "'Women Known for These Acts' through the Rabbinic Lens: A Study of *Hilchot Lesbiut*" in the anthology I edited, *Keep Your Wives Away From Them: Orthodox Women, Unorthodox Desires* (2010).)

Today, decades after that liberating *tikkun leyl Shavuot*, modern Orthodox rabbis who are so inclined are still trying to figure out *halakhic* solutions to the problem of being LGBTQ+ and Orthodox. They debate how we should be treated in communities in which – as Rambam shows – we have already existed for centuries. And when they work within the usual *halakhic* frameworks, by necessity they have to use the language of the sources. This means that new responsa, no matter how supportive of LGBTQ+ Jews the authors wish to be, continue to represent us by one forbidden act, the only identifier for us in the Torah and rabbinic literature. The first 70 pages of Rabbi Fox's article – his *teshuva* bereft of a *she'ela* – fall into this trap.

But then Rabbi Fox swerves. In the very last section of the article, he abruptly sets aside the rabbis' language, their *halakhic* categories, and any source that might be directly relevant to the question of how to reconcile lesbian identity or lesbian sex with traditional *halakha*. He abruptly turns to the Talmudic story (Shabbat 33a) of Rabbi Shimon bar Yochai and his son as they emerge from a cave after many years of hiding, whereupon they are initially offended by ordinary people just living their lives. For Rabbi Fox, this story serves as a parable by which he appeals to readers to treat queer frum women with dignity. He comments:

> We are living in a time when too many great *rabbanim* and *poskim* view Torah through a lens that destroys the lives of gay women (and men). The Gemara is trying to teach us that sometimes, even after many years of deep learning, there is a need to go back into the cave and rethink our approach… You need to open your eyes, without fire, and turn a loving, lifesaving gaze upon Jews who seek to fulfill God's will.

Rabbi Fox's conclusion is open-hearted, humble, compassionate, and attuned to the importance of human experience. This *seifa*, however, is utterly disconnected from the seventy pages of careful, thorough, and learned text that form the *reisha*. The principal approach of the *teshuva* is *halakhic*;

Rabbi Fox's final answer, however, is meta-*halakhic*. What are we to make of this?

For me, the answer is that there is an uncomfortable dissonance between the traditional methods of *halakha*, on the one hand, and the appropriate way of thinking about Orthodox LGBTQ+ Jews, on the other. Although the usual *halakhic* approach will serve us when we need and seek answers on many topics, it will not yield a regard for the humanity and dignity of LGBTQ+ Jews. Orthodox leaders will not find the answers they need for how to include and serve all of their members by turning to the *halakhic* sources. Instead, they must start from a different place: from the *seifa*, as it were. "Gay Women (*Nashim Mesolelot*): A Teshuva" ends in the right place. It is my hope that future rabbis will start where Rabbi Fox ends. Starting with a meta-*halakhic* commitment to the whole person, and the whole community they serve, rabbis will be able to undertake a new process of determining *halakha* when it comes to matters of personal dignity.

Acknowledgements

Thank you to the past, current and future students of Yeshivat Maharat. Your drive to learn and teach Torah inspires me every day. To the leadership of the Yeshiva, thank you for believing in me and in this important project. Rabba Sara, your friendship and leadership mean so much to me and my family. To Rabbi Erin, thank you for shepherding this book to conclusion. Rabbi Weiss, your vision, kindness and love is what drives us all.

To my friends and colleagues who wrote in response, thank you for your scholarship and sensitivity. Your writing situates the *teshuva* inside a robust *halakhic* discourse.

Thank you to my amazing family for putting up with a Shabbat table that does not fit the mold. To my boys for knowing when to laugh and when to take me seriously. Shamma we will have to wait for the second volume…

My mother has modeled for me a life-long commitment to learning and growing. Thank you for all that you gave Paul, Seth and me. I pray that Daddy and Uncle Ivan are proud (and sharing a good joke in *shamayim*).

Beth, your love and support made this possible. The journey of parenting is long with many twists and turns. There is no one else I would rather share it with than you.

—Jeffrey Fox

About the Author

Rabbi Jeffrey S. Fox serves as the Rosh ha-Yeshiva and Dean of Faculty of Yeshivat Maharat. Before coming to the Yeshiva he served as the Rabbi of Kehilat Kesher: The Community Synagogue of Tenafly and Englewood, NJ. He has taught at the Drisha Institute, the Florence Melton Adult Education Center and at Yeshivat Hadar. He received *smicha* as part of the first graduating class of Yeshivat Chovevei Torah. Reb Jeff lives in Riverdale with his wife and four boys.

www.ingramcontent.com/pod-product-compliance
Lightning Source LLC
Chambersburg PA
CBHW020202090426
42734CB00008B/908